Julia

IF YOU ARE
THE SON
OF GOD

Translation from Russian by Rebecca Mildren.
Cover design and layout by My Zion LLC.
All biblical quotations are taken from the NKJV, unless otherwise indicated.

FOREWORD

This book is about love: the love God has for Israel. It describes the tremendous love the Lord holds for the people whom He calls His son and firstborn. It is a reminder that he who touches Israel *touches the apple of His eye.*[1] It illustrates the unchanging nature of the Lord's inviolable love for His people, even though this love may often be hidden from sight behind Israel's more obvious natural existence. It follows, then, that this book is also about faith, for *faith is… the evidence of things not seen.*[2] The inner-workings of God's heart differ greatly from the circumstances our earthly eyes can see, as well as from the conclusions we are able to draw based on them alone. The Lord is teaching us to see through eyes of faith, and to perceive the love He has for Israel, though it often remains invisible.

We live in frighteningly ruthless times, when Israelis living in their own land can still clearly make out the burning stench of the Holocaust in the air. Yeshua prophesied of this time when He said, *'Because lawlessness will abound, the love of many will grow cold,'*[3] and this includes callousness towards even those most dear to Him. For reasons that defy earthly logic, at this critical juncture in time the tragic visible circumstances of Jewish history are paradoxically becoming the source of a rise in hatred and anti-Semitism, the basis for additional accusations that the people of Israel themselves are to blame for everything. The Lord is calling you to turn away from the things which are seen

---

[1] Zech. 2:8
[2] Heb. 11:1
[3] Mat. 24:12

in order to seek His mind, His Spirit. *For what man knows the things of a man except the spirit of the man which is in him? Even so no one knows the things of God except the Spirit of God.* The Lord desires for those who have *received… the Spirit who is from God*[4] to judge Him not according to outward appearances, but to strive to discover and know His heart.

There is absolutely no doubt – it is a truth that requires no discussion or argument – that the people of Israel are in desperate need of repentance and a living relationship with the living God. There is likewise no doubt that God has repeatedly punished the Jewish people for their sins and disobedience. This book is NOT about this indisputable aspect of our history, however, but about something entirely different: **it is about God's plan and the love hidden beneath the surface of this plan.** If you were to speak on the topic of a father and how he loves his son, it does not necessarily follow that you are suggesting his son is perfect, never does anything wrong, or that the father never punishes him. In exactly the same way, God's love for a people whom He has called His son, and equally so His plan for this people, does not necessarily need to be weighed relative to their sin or righteousness. As you read this book, take note of how none of the Bible stories through which the Lord revealed to me the destiny of Israel are connected with the flaws of the stories' heroes. None of these people did anything special to merit being the hero. It was not by their choice, it was not a reward or a penalty: it was the plan of God. In the same way, the things happening to Israel are not a reward or a penalty; they are the outworking of God's plan for His people. In this sense it is very important that in opening this book you remember that **it is about the character of God, and not about the character of Israel. It is not so much a revelation about Israel as it is a revelation God gave of Himself and His heart, a revelation of His love for His people.**

In that sense, this book is not merely about Israel. It is about **what is taking place in God's heart when *the one whom He loves* is suffering.** This word is for each one of us, since we live

---

[4] 1 Cor. 2:11-12

in a world where suffering is ever increasing and the external, visible events we witness are daily becoming more and more frightening. The tragedies shaking our countries can no longer be taken in; they are beyond all human comprehension. With each fire that breaks out, the scorched and charred bodies and souls again demand an answer from believers to that most tormenting of questions, the question that was distinctly audible in the groans that rose up over Beslan, that has chafed the hearts of the Holocaust survivors, and that my fellow countrymen still ask each other today with each successive explosion: Where is God? Why does He remain silent? How could He allow all this? A great number of the children who perished in Beslan were from believing families. They attended congregation and Sunday school. How could God have allowed such a thing to happen? How could He not have answered their prayers? How could He abandon those who trusted in Him even in their last moments? In this sense, this book is also about faith, for *faith is the substance of things hoped for, the evidence of things not seen.*[5] The Lord is teaching us to see with eyes of faith and recognize His love at the moment when everything around us appears to be screaming the opposite. *For what man knows the things of a man except the spirit of the man which is in him? Even so no one knows the things of God except the Spirit of God.*[6] The inner workings of His heart differ greatly from visible circumstances, as well as from the conclusions many arrive at based on them. The Lord desires for those who have *received the Spirit who is from God* to judge him not according to outward appearances, but to seek to know His heart and see His tears that are hidden from the eyes of the world.

I would now like to say some words of acknowledgement to the people so very precious to me, without whom this book would not have been possible. My first thanks belong to my dear husband, Victor. Without his love, without our long talks and prayers, these pages would never have become a reality. I thank God for my priceless friend Bella and for all those like her who have supported me in prayer all these years while this book was

---

[5] Heb. 11:1
[6] 1 Cor. 2:11

being written. I am grateful to the Lord for the open heart and gentle participation of the Jerusalem-based Messianic Pastor, Brother Reuven Berger, and for our friendship with him. His deep and genuine relationship with God became an excellent test for my book, a special form of spiritual proof-reading. My warm gratitude also belongs to believer and poetess Brenda Giles, whose faithfulness and support were the tangible expression of God's faithfulness and support to me. I am incredibly thankful to God for all those who participated in and supported the project of translating this book into other languages, in particular that He made collaboration possible with Rebecca Mildren, an outstanding and insightful translator, thanks to whom my book now appears in beautiful English. To conclude, I would like to quote from a letter I received from Brenda Dauber, a sister very dear to me, with whom I became acquainted in the summer of 2003 at a Messianic conference. God touched her and her husband Lyle through the word God gave me concerning His love for Israel, and they decided to subsidize the English translation of this book – the book of a person, whom they had seen for the first time in their lives. I want to thank them here from the bottom of my heart: dear Brenda and Lyle, this translation became possible only thanks to your open hearts! This is what Brenda wrote to me, recalling the circumstance of our meeting: "Your letter this morning makes me think back on the conference, also, and realize that for such a long time the accuser of the brethren has been paying close attention to your message (book) and has been trying to defeat its publication among the nations. I read this week... that the Lord will "remove the shame" of Israel. When the world sees that the God of Israel is the mighty God of Hosts, all our shame will be removed..."

Finally, I would like to address those of my readers who have not yet met God, have not yet come to know Him, and for whom Israel's suffering is one of the obstacles on the path to this meeting. I hope and pray that through these pages the Lord will not only help you better understand what is happening to Israel, but will also open up His heart so you can see into it, so that you can perceive the enormous love, the countless tears, that are

6

invisible to the world. Throughout the pages of this book He calls you into His inner room where He wants to open up His heart up to you, reveal His love for Israel, and reconfirm His love for you.

For Zion's sake I will not keep silent, for Jerusalem's sake I will not remain quiet, **till her righteousness shines out like the dawn...** (Is 62:1 NIV)

Thus says the LORD, **Israel is My son, My firstborn.** (Ex. 4:22)

PROLOGUE

...Take now your son, your only son...,
whom you love, and go to the land of Moriah; and
offer him there as a burnt offering...(Gen 22:2)

The secret things belong to the LORD our God: but those things which are revealed belong to us and to our children forever, that we may do all the words of this law.[7] This link between the "secret things", that which yet belongs only to the Lord, and the "things revealed", that which in His kindness He has shown so that we could know and fulfill His Word, has not grown fainter over time. By God's great mercy this connection between things secret and things revealed is continually active, utterly alive. I am not implying that the amount of revelation available to mankind is progressively multiplying, for in no way is the movement of God's Spirit linearly progressive, but rather, even today the living Lord speaks with us through His living Word, continuing to reveal *the secret things*.

It is with this in mind that I ask you to visualize that mountain, the location of one of the strangest events in the history of Israel. See the aging father, who with his own hands binds his beloved son and who, with his very own hands, lays him on the altar. Knife in hand, he has already stretched out his arm to slay him, but... halted by a voice from heaven, he looks up and sees a ram caught in a thicket by its horns, which he then sacrifices as a burnt offering in the place of the son originally intended for this sacrifice. When from the lofty height of millenniums afterwards, we look back down at this mountain and at these three figures,

---

[7] Deut. 29:29

8

our hearts literally quiver with the awareness of near-physical contact with this special *secret*, with the foretaste of some incredibly important and only partially understood, not yet *revealed*, mystery of God. Here we brush up against something that without a doubt still belongs to God, but the incomprehensible inner turbulence, which agitates us to the point of outward trembling, testifies that this picture is like some episode from His forethoughts and plans for the history of the world, fashioned for our viewing. This long ago slaying of the sacrificial lamb, which took place perhaps even before the beginning of time but somehow still resounds today, exceeds all bounds of history, time and the passing world. Something incredibly important is taking place here. Something is taking shape against the backdrop of all the long ages of human history: an unsolved mystery stands behind these actions. Are you aware that every year during the holiday of *Rosh Hashanah*, at the beginning of every Jewish year, this story entitled *"Akedah"*, the story of the binding and sacrifice of Isaac, is read in the synagogues? Why? What is so important for us that every time we enter a new year of our earthly walk, we again look at this story? Why did the father have to sacrifice his son? Who was this son, laid on the altar by his father? And this ram, caught in the thicket by his horns – what does he symbolize? I found an interesting passage in the *Haggadah:* "I heard from behind the Heavenly Veil these words: 'Not Isaac, but the ram predestined for the burnt offering.'"[8]

There are some chapters in the Bible which are almost humanly unbearable, and the twenty-second chapter of the Book of *Bereshit*[9] is definitely one of them. I was already a mother when I came to the faith and though I was a believer and had already discovered and fallen in love with God's Word, when I opened the Bible I would hurry through that chapter. It was much like in childhood, when you flip quickly past particular pages in some favorite book: though you know what is written on them, you wish you didn't and you are afraid to once again stumble across them and be pained by their contents. I would make every effort

---

[8] *Haggadah: Tales, proverbs, sayings of the Talmud and Midrash*
[9] The Hebrew name for the Book of Genesis

to skip as quickly as possible over these pages, afraid to be hurt anew by even the smallest glance at the terrifying story of how, in obedience to God, Abraham took his son and led him to Mount Moriah to present him there as a burnt offering. Much time had to pass before I could read and reread this story, pray about it and meditate on it, and before I allowed the Lord to speak to me through it. It was a long time before I had the courage to imagine those two, father and son, together ascending to the summit where in obedience to God each would have to fulfill his own task and experience his own torment, sacrifice and death process, where they would reach that which was to become the personal climax for each of them. *The LORD God is my strength; …He will make me to walk upon mine high places,*[10] and truly the verses of this entire chapter are like steps in a staircase ascending to that unattainable height to which a person can be elevated by God alone. They lead us from the first step in which Abraham, in response to the call of God and not yet knowing what lay ahead of him, says, *'Here I am,'*[11] to that final, inconceivable step in which *Abraham stretched out his hand and took the knife to slay his son…*[12]

For whom was it more difficult in this narrative – for the father, or the son? For the one who with his own handled his infinitely dear son to the altar, or for the one who, unawares, was led to be slain? It is interesting that the Scriptures give us a detailed account of only the actions, not saying a word about what was transpiring in the souls of those they describe. This of course does not mean that our feelings are not important to Him. The Lord who was tempted in all sorrows is with us in our suffering, but the bottom line, that which is entered into the heavenly annals, is our obedience to Him and not how much pain it cost us. At the same time, one can surely guess what was going on in the heart of the father as he walked down the path, knowing for what and for whom he *took the fire in his hand.*[13] Abraham knew what awaited him, and he knew why he was doing it. Upon

---

[10] Hab. 3:19 (KJV)
[11] Gen. 22:1
[12] Gen. 22:10
[13] Gen. 22:6 *

arriving at the destination he could say, like Yeshua thousands of years later, *"Now My soul is troubled, and what shall I say? 'Father, save Me from this hour'? But for this purpose I came to this hour."*[14] The father knew only too well the reason for going up this mountain, but the son knew nothing. Isaac was obviously perplexed, all the time understanding less and less what was going on and *where the lamb for the burnt offering*[15] was, but despite all this, without a single complaint he continued to follow his father in perfect obedience, perfect trust. *He was led as a lamb to the slaughter.*[16] Picture a boy[17] obediently ascending the mountain behind his father with a heavy load of firewood on his back, not having the slightest inclination of what awaits him there at the top. He loved his father and knew that his father loved him. Least of all could he imagine his father doing anything to him inconsistent with his perception of the fatherly love of which he was the object. Consider what Isaac must have experienced when his father, whose love for him was the unshakeable foundation of his life, started to tie him up and having bound him, laid him on the altar on top of the wood and raised the hand with the knife over him… Imagine the horror in the eyes of your child, if you had done all this to him – horror not even so much in the face of death as the horror of absolute incomprehension of what his adored and adoring father is doing to him and where his love has disappeared to. This horror was fully experienced by the beloved son of Abraham, after which the trial was brought to an end.

This story resonates with a mystery words cannot fully describe. It is the mystery of the father-son relationship, gradually displayed more and more fully for us as the pair continues the journey to the mountaintop. Consider: this is a path down which the father leads his son, a path on which the son starts out as just a son but which he finds ends at the altar. **A path on which, in walking down it, the son *becomes* the lamb, with none other**

---

[14] John 12:27

[15] Gen. 22:7

[16] Is. 53:7

[17] Even if, as according to some accounts, Isaac was already more than thirty, he was still completely submissive to and entirely dependent on his father: in all ways yet a child.

than the father himself leading him to be sacrificed. The one who up until now was simply a beloved son is transformed on this path into the lamb to be offered up by the father. And the most unfathomable, the most torturous, tragic feature in all of this is that the son himself does not yet know about it. He knows that he is the son beloved of his father, but with every step on the path, each taken in complete ignorance, the closer he gets to the altar the more complete his transformation becomes. With a heart reeling from the agony, the father leads the son-lamb to his slaughter. In this is the mystery and secret of the Father's plan, the Father's love, and the Father's election: **the Mystery of Sonship.**

It is generally accepted that Isaac, led by the father to the *mizbeach*, or altar, is a type of the Son of God on the way to His crucifixion: *for God so loved the world, that He gave His only begotten Son...*[18] But is this really so? The outwardly tranquil ascent of Isaac, which for us is filled with such heart-wrenching anguish – the father leading the son who doesn't even suspect that he is to be the sacrificial lamb – is completely absent in the case of Yeshua. The Son sacrificed by the Heavenly Father came consciously and willingly to offer His life on the altar. *'I lay down My life that I may take it again. No one takes it from Me, but I lay it down of Myself.'*[19] He knew He was the Lamb slain from the foundation of the world. He knew the path He was to take. He could see the entire earthly race laid out before Him with its Golgotha finish-line that awaited Him. Most likely, this knowledge made it all the more difficult, but in any case His is a different story, a different election. Isaac, in contrast, submissively followed where his father led, all the time wondering *where the lamb for the burnt offering*[20] was, and not realizing that **he** was to become the lamb.

Isaac is Israel – led to the altar by the Heavenly Father. Israel – who fully knows that he is the beloved son, but who has not yet understood and to whom it has not yet been revealed, that on

---

[18] John 3:16
[19] John 10:17-18
[20] Gen. 22:7

this path his eternally loving Father is transforming him into the sacrificial lamb and leading him to be slain. This is not treachery or deception, but the mystery and secret of sonship, of God's election purposes... the mystery of God's love. Israel – to whom the plan of the Father is not revealed and is yet unclear and who, frequently bewildered, follows where his Father leads him. Israel – who is predestined to walk down the entire length of the path, almost to the very end, and to experience all the horror of confusion about what has happened to the Father and His love for him... before the hand stretched over him with the knife is stopped. Israel – whom God calls His son, His firstborn, and who as the son is chosen for this very path of sacrifice. In contrast to the Son of God, who from the beginning knew that He had come to earth to die for the sake of others, Israel remains in total ignorance, continually horrified in his inability to comprehend what his Heavenly Father is doing with him, yet walking out the sorrowful path of his election as a sacrifice for the sake of other peoples. This is what the Apostle Paul meant when he wrote to the Gentiles: *Enemies for your sake.*[21]

When people say that everything that has happened to Israel is punishment for their sins and falling away, I think about the story of Abraham and Isaac. Yes, every loving father chastises his son. This is the principle on which the whole Biblical concept of child-raising is built. There is a difference, however, between chastising and what Abraham did. A child might cry and be scared when you punish him and this becomes part of how he views his father, but if you, like Abraham, were to stretch out your hand to slay your son and offer him as a burnt offering, that is not punishment. It is sacrifice. The terror that would appear in the eyes of your child would not only be the fear of death, but the dismay of not being able to understand what has happened to your love. It is highly significant that at each *Rosh Hashanah,* each New Year, this portion *"Akedah"* about the binding of Isaac is read. The people of Israel look at this story with mixed feelings of fear and wonder, understanding that it somehow bears significance to their fate, but are unable to

---

[21] Rom. 11:28

discern the truth: that they are looking into a mirror. This scene, this ascent up the mountain and all that happened there, is like a miniature of our history: the history of the ages, and the history of each year. Even when we ourselves don't understand it, this is the main thing that we have to say for ourselves every time we enter a new year of our history: Our ascent. Our binding. Our sacrifice. Similar to how the Epistle to the Hebrews speaks concerning Levi, we can also say that Israel in the person of Isaac was present at this ascent and altar, for we were *still in the loins of [our] father*[22] when Isaac was supposed to have been offered up as a sacrifice. Bound by the Father, Israel lies on the altar so long as the trial continues.

Within this scene, this prologue not only to the history of Israel but in fact to the entire history of mankind, is encapsulated the entirety of God's design for the ages, His complete plan for humanity. It is not by coincidence that the location where all this takes place was later to become **the main** focal point of God in the visible world. It is the mountain of Moriah, the Temple Mount in Jerusalem, on which the Temple will be built that the Lord will one day fill with His glory. *'God will provide for Himself the lamb for a burnt offering,'*[23] Abraham tells Isaac, and although there on the mountain at first we see only two figures – Abraham and Isaac, father and son – after a time it turns out that there is someone else in the picture: *the ram caught in a thicket by its horns.*[24] The lamb, which God provided for Himself for the burnt offering! Neither Abraham nor we the readers could see how and when he got there; he simply **was** there, and had been from the very beginning. In Jewish sources it says that the ram, this lamb, had already been slain before the creation of the world. This is why each time at the rebirth of the year we read about this story that somehow echoes from beyond the realm of time. In its light we can discern how in God's plan for the salvation of mankind, at first there are two: God, and Israel who is called the son and firstborn, but *in the dispensation of the fullness*

---

[23] Gen. 22:8
[24] Gen. 22:13

of the times[25] it turns out that there is also The Lamb, who from the creation of the world was destined for sacrifice. Remember this portion I quoted earlier from the *Haggadah,* "I heard from behind the Heavenly Veil these words: 'Not Isaac, but the ram predestined for the burnt offering.'" The Lamb slain from the foundation of the world replaces on the altar the one, whom God Himself has called His son and firstborn.

The atoning sacrifice of the Lamb is that foundation of foundations on which the personal faith and salvation of each born-again believer is built, *for the Jew first and also for the Greek;*[26] but the *Akedah* – the sacrifice of Israel, the sacrificial election of Israel in the plan of God – has not yet been fully revealed either to the Jew, or to the Greek. This book attempts to articulate this *secret,* and I pray that the inadequate words of man would be quickened and filled with His Spirit.

---

[25] Eph. 1:10
[26] Rom. 1:16

CHAPTER ONE

God has delivered me to the ungodly, and turned me over
to the hands of the wicked... They gape at me with their mouth,
they strike me reproachfully on the cheek, they gather together
against me... You have hidden their heart from understanding...
You will not exalt them. (Job 16:11,10; 17:4)

Now also many nations have gathered against you, who say,
"Let her be defiled, and let our eye look upon Zion." But they
do not know the thoughts of the LORD, nor do they understand
His counsel... (Mic. 4:11,12)

Not long after I had finished writing my first book, *Why are you*
weeping? Whom are you seeking?[27] which discusses the suffering of
Job, a certain Finnish brother remarked that it should have an
appendix or sequel about Israel. At the time I did not grasp the
significance of what he said, but now I know it was a prophetic
word. I always knew that the story of Job spoke to my past, to
my own experience of sorrow and pain from which, though
embarked upon as a resolute unbeliever, I emerged if not exactly
knowing Him, at least strongly convinced of His existence. What
I didn't know then, however, was that this book was destined to
revisit my future with such pain and sorrow, with the tears and
groanings of my people. *A man can receive nothing unless it has*
been given to him from heaven,[28] and that is why I know for certain

---

[27] Jerusalem: Keren Ahvah Meshihit, Russian edition, 1995.
[28] John 3:27

it was the Lord Himself who filled my heart with this constant pain for Israel that cannot be allayed, this *great sorrow and continual grief* [29] concerning His people. Never would I have ventured to write on this new theme, however, had I not come to believe that together with the prayers and tears, it was from His hand I also received another difficult calling: to not keep silent *for Zion's sake..., for Jerusalem's sake..., till her righteousness shines out like the dawn...* [30]

The Lord has been guiding me towards this for a long time now. In all honesty, it has taken me years even to dare come near this subject. I just couldn't bring myself to approach a theme so full of anguish, hurt and heaviness. It encompasses so much pain and so many tears that any word spoken, no matter how good the intentions, could only serve to deepen the wound of those already injured beyond measure... if not received directly from the Lord. I was given the grace to write earlier about the suffering of Job, and I know that through it He has touched and continues to touch many lives, comforting those in distress and restoring the brokenhearted even as he comforted and restored Job. However, the first thing He revealed to me through Job was the futility of trying to help and console the afflicted in fleshly strength or with the words of man. That is why it is with the weight of such responsibility and even fear that I shift my focus from the suffering of a biblical character to that of living people, my people – to the suffering of Israel.

The years lived out here in Jerusalem have taught me to measure time the way Israelis do: not by hours, but from one news program to the next. The explosions of near-daily terrorist attacks, the moans of the wounded and the unreal grief of those burying their dead, the news reports that begin by reading the names of those who have been murdered in the past twenty-four hours, the pervading hatred and condemnation with all of its glaring injustices making up the continual backdrop of our lives – all this has placed me, as a believer, face to face with the question of the true meaning of God's election of my people. To

---

[29] Rom. 9:2
[30] Is. 62:1

what end were we chosen by God? For what, in history and eternity, were a people chosen whose earthly lot always seems to be... suffering?

It is not within our earthly ability to fully open this scroll, rolled up and sealed by the hand of God Himself, entitled "The Mystery of Israel". All that we see from here we see, in the words of Paul, as if *in a mirror, dimly,* only there will we see *face to face.*[31] Far too many of my people, having asked this question of God, have been crushed by the weight of the unimaginable affliction through which Israel has gone and is still going through today. The question of our calling and election – the place of the chosen people within the plan of God and the purpose to which we were destined – was, indeed, too agonizing a question for me, but today the certainty of His commission to talk about it is stronger within me than my reservations. Therefore, even while reminding myself that it will be *in a mirror, dimly,* despite this I humbly take up the task before me. Approaching His mystery of Israel as one would a mountain peak flaming with fire, and uttering as Moses once did at the base of the mountain, *'I am exceedingly afraid and trembling,'*[32] in profound weakness I pray today that the One who has entrusted me with this word would Himself also empower me to present it.

Have you considered My servant?

Let us remember how the story of Job starts, the story of his testing and suffering. *'Have you considered My servant Job?'*[33] the Lord asks at the very beginning of the book. To whom is He speaking? To one of the heavenly host? Not at all! He is speaking to... Satan! Everything that happens to Job in the first two chapters of the book is caused by Satan, and he is doing it not only with the consent of God but, what is more, upon His recommendation! Bizarre, is it not? But when we see the Lord Himself pointing Job out to Satan, we begin to grasp Job's

---

[31] 1 Cor. 13:12
[32] Heb. 12:21
[33] Job 1:8

unique election: God's special notice of Job reveals that he is handpicked by the Almighty for the starring role in the Book of Job.

In this context, thinking back on Israel's anguished history, you can almost hear God saying to Satan long ago, "Have you considered My servant Israel?" Satan's response, the dialogue which we witness twice between him and God in the first and second chapters of Job, could be used as an epigraph for our history. *'Does Job fear God for nothing? ...stretch out Your hand and touch all that he has, and he will surely curse You to Your face! ...stretch out Your hand now, and touch his bone and his flesh, and he will surely curse You to Your face!'*[34] Time after time history has borne witness to this ghastly satanic scene; any persecution against a Jewish person begins with touching *all that he has*, and almost unavoidably leads to touching *his bone and his flesh*.

Why does the One who loves us remain silent?

Why does He let all this happen?

Why do You stand afar off, O LORD? Why do You hide in times of trouble?[35]

Is it possible, could it really be that You are simply trying us? Could all of our bloody history be just a test provoked by Satan's malicious, perfidious slander, "Does Israel *fear God for nothing?*"

It was with such questions that my meditations about Job first began. "How," nearly choking with indignation after reading the Book of Job for the first time, not yet a believer, "how could it possibly be for the sake of a test that God would unleash all these sufferings on Job, who hadn't even a trace of sin?" I wasn't the one who "dug up" the answers to my questions, but the Lord offered them to me Himself by unlocking the Book of Job for me. He allowed me to see the path Job traveled through these chapters, how Job went from being a man with rent *garments* to

---

[34] Job 1:9,11; 2:5
[35] Ps. 10:1

one possessing a rent *heart,*[36] and about how He Himself answered this sad, torn heart just how He always answers the humble and broken-hearted. I am convinced that similar to the case of Job, it is not humanly possible to fully grasp the significance of the sufferings of Israel. I am simply writing what the Lord has revealed to me and I believe that His voice, not mine, will touch your hearts.

The insight on suffering the Lord initially revealed to me through Job was that the true question in all suffering is not "for what sin is He doing this to me?" but "for what purpose?" But, whereas in the past I had always focused on Job himself and his relationship with God (the comforter-friends with their opinions and the issues of man's judgment then being of only secondary importance to me when compared to the hugely significant interchange between God and a human heart), I now want for us to look at the history of Job not from within, but from without. We will try to accept that the answer "for the purpose of..." is not restricted to the life and heart of the one chosen to undergo suffering. The suffering of Job was intended to a great extent for those who were near him, who witnessed his suffering, condemned him in that suffering and who, in the end, through his suffering came to know the love and mercy of God for the first time. Job calls them *miserable comforters*[37] and *worthless physicians,*[38] and their presence truly seems almost useless; but at the same time, and though not even conscious of it, Job suffered for them as well, **for the purpose of** their life also being changed. This is the perspective we will now explore.

The apple of His eye

There was a time when I too was a *worthless physician* and just as self-confidently as a comforter of Job, diagnosed the ailments of Israel. When eleven years ago we arrived in Jerusalem having just come to the faith and just discovered the One who is *the way,*

---

[36] Joel 2:13
[37] Job 16:2
[38] Job 13:4

the truth and the life,[39] I was naively convinced that it was enough to simply share about this Way with all who didn't know… and immediately the light would dawn for everyone. "What right do you have?" one of our lady friends demanded of me. Before coming to Israel she had considered herself a Christian but here, as she put it, she came to understand that not only did she not have the right to teach these people anything, these men and women who had paid for their own country and their own way with blood and tears, but she didn't even have the right to see the truth differently than they saw it. She had no right to know another truth or way, otherwise she would be treating them dishonorably. I was too overflowing with Him (and myself?) to understand this. If He was the Truth, how could I give up my right to the Truth?

Years went by. It was only when I began to write the final, seventh chapter of my book about Job, the chapter directed at *my brethren, my countrymen according to the flesh,*[40] that the Lord stopped me. It was then for the first time He spoke to me about it Himself. He touched my heart and it seemed that not from my eyes but from my heart, rivers of tears began to burst forth, forever setting those days apart for me. This was to be His first conversation with me about Israel. He began to teach me (me, a Jewish believer and Israeli!) **His** love for His people. Convicting and chastising me for lightly esteeming *the apple of His eye,*[41] He showed me just how much the suffering of His people weighed in His sight, and that if it *were fully weighed… it would be heavier than the sand of the sea.*[42] He showed me how displeasing to Him are both the Jewish and Gentile people who so readily and presumptuously analyze this suffering, who are so convinced of their own merit and superiority, and who think they know the real reason the people of Israel suffer.

---

[39] John 14:6
[40] Rom. 9:3
[41] Zech. 2:8
[42] Job 6:3

Deadly seeds

No, I am not taking it upon myself to describe here the history of Christian anti-Semitism. Volumes and volumes would be needed in order to fit all the blood-spattered pages necessary to tell the gruesome history from which, I might add, my people learned only too well about Christianity. Just as in the gloomy Russian fairy-tale where the black, empty field turned out to be sown with seeds that in the morning grew into dragons, from those deadly seeds planted during the first centuries of the Church's history, the monster of anti-Semitism sprang up in the centuries that followed, from the Crusaders to the Holocaust. I do not intend to write about these "dragons"; thanks be to God, the pages of this dark history have already begun to be written not only by Jewish authors but also, through tears of repentance, by true believers in the One in whose Name so much outrage and brutality was carried out.

As a believer in Yeshua, it is very important to me to understand what these seeds were that yielded such a frightening harvest. What exactly went wrong? What was the reason for this monstrous perversion of attitude, this seemingly inexplicable hatred of those who later became the followers of Yeshua towards those to whom He initially revealed Himself? Do we not, having loved, not also begin to love all that somehow is associated with our beloved? Having come to love Him, should they not have also loved everything connected with His earthly life, and first and foremost His people, the ones among whom He lived and whom He loved? Why did everything turn out completely the other way around and instead, His people became especially hated, despised and persecuted by Christians? Why?

To my shame and horror, I realize that if we dig deeply enough, it becomes clear that the suffering of Israel during the first centuries after Yeshua was what helped the Church find a theological base for her hatred and contempt. No, of course suffering was not the reason for this hatred, but in Israel's troubles and misery, early Christianity uncovered the main evidence and confirmation that Israel was rejected by God and that the Church, the "true", "heavenly", "new" Israel, would forevermore be in the place of the "chosen people". Consider: this is an extremely frightening turn of events! Even nonbelievers perceive Christianity as a religion of mercy and compassion, but it was Christians that ended up not only being the ones who didn't help or show compassion to Israel in their sorrows, but who far too soon themselves began to hate, persecute and kill. *For they persecute the ones You have struck, and talk of the grief of those You have wounded.*[43]

'He who is without sin among you, let him throw a stone at her first,'[44] Yeshua said of the woman caught in adultery. Though she was caught in outright sin and surrounded by scribes and Pharisees who led lawfully pious lives, when confronted not one of them considered himself blameless enough to throw a stone at her. These are the very ones, incidentally, that Christianity has declared the epitome of religious self-satisfaction and self-righteousness. Scarcely a century later, we find Israel tormented and spat upon, encircled by her Christian brethren. All equally convinced of their own righteousness and her sinfulness, one after another and in complete contradiction to the words and spirit of the Teacher... they begin to stone her. We will yet return to the issue of guilt, to the "adultery" of Israel, but leaving this aside for the time being, let's shudder together at what our eyes are seeing, at this spectacle of ruthless lynching (carried out in the very presence of the true Judge, no less), at these stones flying at us, hurled by those who to others preached love and mercy.

I want to repeat myself clearly: we are not going to deal with the reasons for and meaning of Israel's suffering just yet; this is a theme for chapters to follow. We are speaking now only of the attitude of Christians to this suffering. This attitude was formed in the first centuries of Christian history, necessitating our investigation begin here. Before the Church began to persecute Israel herself (these persecutions being tomorrow's "dragons"),

---

[43] Ps. 69:26
[44] John 8:7

she diligently sowed her field with the following fateful theological seeds: if the people of Israel are suffering so horribly, this means that God has punished and rejected them and in view of this, they deserve nothing but contempt from those who have rightfully taken their place. In his treatise "Dialogue with Trypho" Justin Martyr declared that all the sufferings of the Jewish people are the righteous punishment of God for the death of Christ, and this became one of the first stones cast at Israel. When speaking of the expulsion of Jewish residents from Jerusalem, the devastation of the Land and the burned Jewish towns, he didn't hesitate to label all these afflictions only the just deserts of the Righteous One's murderers. For some reason he failed to recall Stephen's prayer about forgiving the men stoning him, or the prayer of Yeshua Himself while on the cross. The following are some additional voices:

- Irenaeus, Bishop of Lyon (circa 177): "The Jews are separated from the grace of God."

- Tertullian of Carthage (160-230 C.E.): in his treatise "Answer to the Jews," he declared that God had rejected the Jewish people and replaced them with Christians.

- Gregory, Bishop of Nyssa in Cappadocia (died in 394): "The Jews are a brood of vipers, enemies of all that is good."

Sorting through all the stones cast at Israel by the early Church fathers could take, alas, almost an eternity. My goal here, however, is not to examine the dragons of Christian anti-Semitism, but the seeds sown in the very beginning during the very first few hundred years of Christian history. Already in the second century we can see a doctrine formed that can be briefly summarized in the following manner: the Church is the embodiment of the true people of God, the "new Israel", while the Jewish people are to be looked upon as an apostate nation, stripped of their election and punished for the sin of not accepting the Messiah, accused of being "sellers of Christ" and "Christ-killers". God has rejected Israel, and from now on their place is to be occupied by the Church. All the blessings, the promises, all that up until then had been the possession of Israel, now belonged to the Church: God, the Bible, the Promised Land, election, salvation, the Kingdom of God, and so on. Of all the promises in the *Tenach*,[45] only the curses are generously left to our people by the Church.

This calls to mind the children's fable about a fox and a hare: the fox had a hut made from ice, and the hare had a little straw house. The fox's ice hut melts and the hare takes him in, only to find that the fox kicks him out and takes his home. This is approximately what happened with Israel and Christianity, and so rapidly as the second century, at that. In Justin Martyr's treatise we find his "biblical" grounds for such a usurpation. Commenting (interestingly enough, the first among Christian authors to do so) on the story of Noah and his sons found at the end of Genesis chapter nine, he points out the verse, *may God enlarge Japheth,* **and may he dwell in the tents of Shem**,[46] as a prophetic word about how in the future Japheth, the Gentile nations that have received Christianity, in his understanding, would seize the tents of Shem, i.e. Israel. I would like to suggest that the original meaning of this verse did not in any way assume an eviction of Shem from these tents any more than the hare would assume that in letting in the homeless fox, he soon would find himself out in the street. The interpretation of this Christian commentator, however, only served to legitimize the process of Israel's exclusion from the plan and blessings of God, which at that time was already moving ahead at full speed. It is understandable that in the framework of this doctrine the sufferings of Israel came in very handy. They acted as additional proof of Israel's rejection and downfall and consequently were seen as an especially weighty argument in favor of the just rights of Christianity to take their place.

The more terrible the troubles and trials that besought Israel, the more justified the Church became in her own eyes. It is not a coincidence that the point at which the new religion broke with its Jewish roots, though identified approximately from the time

---

[45] The "Old Testament", or the Jewish Scriptures. The acronym "TeNaCH" (תנ״ך) stands for the Torah (the Law), the Neviim (the Prophets), and the Ktuvim (the Writings).
[46] Gen. 9:27

of the Jerusalem Council, became more than distinct especially during our periods of distress, particularly in 70 C.E. with the fall of Jerusalem and the destruction of the Temple, and the years of 132-135 C.E. with the Bar-Kochba revolt and the Roman repressions that followed. Every time things were going badly for Israel, the Church celebrated. In these new and ever increasing troubles Christianity saw all the more fresh confirmation that God had in fact rejected His people… in exactly the same way Job's comforters perceived his sufferings as the sign that God had punished and rejected Job. But they were wrong!

Suffering – a spectator sport?

Once again, it is time to turn to the Book of Job. The insights I want to share here are relatively new to me, and God pointed them out specifically in relation to the suffering of Israel. As I meditated on Job, at the touch of the Creator's hand verses came to life, in the same way it happens every time the Lord speaks. My heart was pierced for the first time by lines from the same text that I had read and re-read continuously but had failed to notice before. I will begin with that tragic lesson taught by the Book of Job which I am sure many believers have had the chance to experience at some point in their lives: the minute you are faced with some calamity, you are bound to appear in the eyes of believing brothers and sisters, even those sympathetic to you, as undergoing punishment from God. It is a common tendency for believers to think, "For some reason God allowed this to happen. *If it is not He, who else could it be?*[47]"

People who don't know God, whose lives are confined to the material world and built exclusively around it, are limited to seeing a situation from the strictly physical, tangible perspective. They refrain from superimposing a spiritual overlay to the

[47] Job 9:24

spectacle of suffering. For them, the grief of a fellow human is reason for compassion at the hands of "good" people, indifference from the not-so-good or in the worst-case scenario, evil glee and malicious gloating on the part of one's enemies. The "worldly" seem to get by just fine without all the tangential spiritualized elucidations. Those who live with a certainty *of things not seen,*[48] however, perceive every situation (and rightfully so) as a letter of the living God written in invisible ink. Upon certain events being brought to their attention, this sort of people can rarely withstand the temptation to "read aloud" that letter which was not addressed to them, and to debate that supposed guilt which incurred such grave punishment. It is therefore vital that believers in particular understand that although even the most tragic situations *work together for good to those who love God*[49] and that from every circumstance we can and must emerge closer to God, difficult circumstances dispatched as punishment are not as common as we tend to think. Even then, however, when what we are witnessing is truly punishment sent from God, this is still a private conversation between God and the one He is addressing, not by any means intended for onlookers and their critical observations.

Let's go back to our story now and remember what it says. Job lived an exceptionally blameless and God-fearing life; the Scriptures verify this for us from the very first lines. As long as everything in his life was prosperous, in his own eyes and in the eyes of those around him (friend and foe alike, right on down to Satan) he was seen as a man unusually blessed by the Almighty, especially close to Him and even, in some sense, God's representative on the earth. *'After my words they did not speak again... They waited for me as for the rain... I chose the way for them, and sat as chief; so I dwelt as a king in the army, as one who comforts mourners.'*[50] Conversely, when troubles and testings all of a sudden swirled around him, everyone without exception until the appearance of Elihu saw this as God's punishment. *'Remember now, who ever perished being innocent? Or where were the*

---

[48] Heb. 11:1
[49] Rom. 8:28
[50] Job 29:22-25

upright ever cut off?'[51] Unexpectedly, Job is not only transformed overnight from a successful man into a man beset by overwhelming grief, but what is much more terrible, yesterday's man of God respected by all is today suddenly rejected as a sinner, an outcast, one thought to be abandoned by God. *'But He has made me a byword of the people, and I have become one in whose face men spit.'*[52] *'Even young children despise me; I arise, and they speak against me. All my close friends abhor me, and those whom I love have turned against me.'*[53]

This acutely bitter sensation of rejection and disgrace, this dreadful realization that in the eyes of bystanders all that is happening to him is the indisputable sign of God's retribution for his evidently multitudinous sins – this is what turns out to be the most excruciating, the most unbearable of all Job's trials. As the book progresses, he speaks out more and more about this, and the physical torment and the sorrow over the loss of loved ones is eclipsed by the horror of unjust condemnation and universal contempt. *'He has cast me into the mire, and I have become like dust and ashes.'*[54] In this sense, the Book of Job is not even so much about the hardships that have come upon him as it is about how extraordinarily difficult (even more difficult than physical suffering!) it is for the one who only yesterday was overshadowed with God's visible blessing to bear this apparent rejection. Up until the very end of the book and his meeting with the Lord, Job tries but can't comprehend the reason for this abrupt major change and why he, upright and God-fearing, has been delivered by God *to the ungodly, and turned… over to the hands of the wicked.*[55]

---

[51] Job 4:7
[52] Job 17:6
[53] Job 19:18-19
[54] Job 30:19
[55] Job 16:11

A lesson from semiotics

Many years ago while studying at the Tartu University in Estonia, I sat in on lectures on the then popular and simultaneously infamous theme of semiotics. Not that this knowledge turned out to be very useful later in my believing life, but recently I happened to remember the first lecture with perfect clarity. The professor started by drawing two circles on the board. "This is the message-sender and this is the recipient," he said. "In the understanding of semiotics, text" – he then drew a zig-zag line joining these two spots – "is communication conveyed by a sender to a receiver," i.e. not just text in the strict sense of the word, but any cultural phenomenon can also be referred to as "text". (This is the way I understood it; I don't recommend using this description as an academic definition). The text sent must not only be received, but also read – decoded or deciphered, so to speak. Naturally, somewhere along this path it is possible that distortions or incorrect deciphering will occur. The recipient of the text might read into it not entirely what, or entirely not what, the message-sender wanted to convey. One of the tasks of a cultural historian is to faithfully decipher the cultural "texts" of past centuries, in order to read into them the exact meaning with which their "authors" invested them.

I remember little of semiotics except for that first lecture, and I don't know if anyone has looked at the story of Job from the standpoint of the semiotic concept. If not, it really is a shame because in my opinion, we have here a perfectly typical example of just such a distortion in "reading", or an inaccurate deciphering and interpretation of a "text". Let's attempt to grasp the huge disparity between how the Author "wrote" this story and how it was "read" by the witnesses surrounding Job. In the first two chapters of the book, the Lord allows Satan to test someone especially near and dear to His heart, in this way producing our tragic "Story of Job". In all the following chapters, throughout which we hear the voice of his friends (up until the appearance of Elihu in chapter thirty-two), we find nothing other than a distorted reading of this original story. The Book of

Job records their wrong interpretation of the misery and sufferings of Job. While the people around Job read what was happening to him as God's punishment for his sins, we who know what was said in the first lines of the book listen with ever-increasing bewilderment to all these accusing speeches. When at one point Job, not able to contain himself, bitterly says to his friends, *'But I have understanding as well as you; I am not inferior to you,'*[56] and later, *'What you know, I also know; I am not inferior to you,'*[57] it is clear to the one who read the book from the beginning that He is speaking the truth. We know that not only in his own eyes but in the eyes of God as well, Job truly excels his comforters in his fear of God and uprightness. Without a doubt, God had something He wanted to do in Job's heart, which was infected at first with both self-righteousness and self-sufficiency; however, of those sins which his friends take such delight in accusing him, Job is clearly and unmistakably innocent. (*'Is not your wickedness great, and your iniquity without end? For you have taken pledges from your brother for no reason, and stripped the naked of their clothing. You have not given the weary water to drink, and you have withheld bread from the hungry... You have sent widows away empty, and the strength of the fatherless was crushed.'*[58]) Moreover, if these comforters, who are totally unaware of God's take on what is happening, are more than convinced of his sinfulness, *'Know therefore that God exacts from you less than your iniquity deserves,'*[59] then it is critical for us to note for the purposes of our further discussion that their guilty verdict is based **exclusively** on the evidence of his misfortune, which they declare to be the punishment of God, and which God informed us from the very beginning of the story that such was not the case at all.

Note that Job himself, unlike we who have the benefit of reading the prologue (and who knows nothing of semiotics), isn't sure of the purposes and plans of God. With all of his tattered soul, with all of his tortured heart feeling the injustice of his comforters'

---

[56] Job 12:3
[57] Job 13:2
[58] Job 22:5-9
[59] Job 11:6

opinions, he flinches from each foregone "conclusion" as if being whipped by them. Once I read a story about a man who, cutting his fingernails down to the quick and armed in this peculiar way, his flesh left without the usual protection and therefore incredibly sensitive, could break into safes by being able to differentiate between the correct and incorrect number on a combination lock. In the same way, a person overtaken by such sorrow finds himself to be naked as it were, stripped perfectly bare of his or her usual protective covering and as a result, incredibly sensitive to any lie or falsehood. As the book goes on it is this false construal of events about which Job all the more cries out to God, hoping and trusting that His reading of the story would differ from that of man's. *'Do You have eyes of flesh? Or do You see as man sees?'*[60]

From the standpoint of today's discussion, is this not virtually the most important lesson we need to gain from this book? That God sees not as man sees, and that the gap between His perspective and man's is not only glaring, but specifically and distinctly pointed out to us? Not one, not two, but three gazes are fixed on Job: the human eyes of his contemporaries from within the story who are reading the events as a tale of sin and God's retribution; the view from Heaven, with full awareness of the pre-history and the true meaning of this tragic text; and ours, the prospect from the outside, the view of the reader to whom, through the story of Job, the Lord is teaching to distinguish between man's interpretation and God's. Only at the story's end do the direct participants receive the first-hand refutation of the false interpretation fought so desperately by Job. It is not by chance, however, that you and I are shown **from the very beginning** the heavenly prologue (such an unexpectedly theatrical preface, so uncharacteristic for a book in the *Tenach*), from the first lines assuring us of the righteousness of Job. Even if somehow someone doesn't quite fully comprehend all that is taking place, this prologue, this conversation between God and Satan, is there to testify beyond a shadow of a doubt that the whole business has nothing to do with punishment.

---

[60] Job 10:4

At the end of the book it is once again confirmed to us that the interpretation of Job's comforters is incorrect. We learn this from Elihu, who acts as God's messenger *(also against his three friends his wrath was aroused, because they had found no answer, and yet had condemned Job[61])*, as well as from the Author of the story Himself who similar to Elihu says that His *wrath is aroused* against the friends of Job that they *'have not spoken of Me what is right, as My servant Job has.'*[62] On top of all this, however, the Spirit of God took pains so that unlike the immediate participants of this story, we the readers would be assured from the very first verses that the reason for Job's sufferings could in no way be construed as punishment. It seems that it was very important to the Author of the book that the reader remember this throughout the duration of all these long-winded speeches filled with condemnation and accusations, just in case they began to seem persuasive at some point. In this sense, the story of Job is not simply a good example but God's conscientiously built illustration of how wide the chasm is between the view of God and the view of man, of how differently one and the same thing can be seen from earth and from heaven, and of how far from God's truth man's interpretation can be.

No neutral territory

We are now left to make that final step, which is to call things as they are. There is a simple spiritual principle which few, unfortunately, take seriously. The majority of people prefer to see themselves rather generously, as open-minded people, perhaps. In our day and age, however, the world that not so long ago seemed to be so multi-colored is now starting to manifest itself more and more as distinctly black and white. This principle, formulated in such an amazingly simple way by Yeshua, *'he who is not with Me is against Me,'*[63] is also becoming all the time more and more evident. There is no longer any neutral

---

[61] Job 32:3
[62] Job 42:7
[63] Mat. 12:30

territory or "compassionate" judgment: all that is not white is black, everyone that is not of God is of the devil, and everything behind which we do not find God – we find our Adversary.

Once I had a truly terrifying experience. A person who was very dear to us was dying from cancer and literally on his deathbed. He came to God, however, through the testimony of my husband and afterwards miraculously began to be healed of his illness. Sadly, he was seduced into a hideous cult. (Curiously enough, since that time I have never heard of that cult again and I have the feeling that Satan thought it up and called it into existence with the sole purpose to *deceive, if possible, even the elect*,[64] and to draw away this brother.) At one point we felt that something not good was happening with him, and we tried to talk with him about it but he evaded all questions, avoided conversation, and wouldn't look us in the eyes. He remained this way, avoiding eye contact, until once when talking with me he looked me directly in the face… and I cringed. I will never forget that icy, sinister hatred that flashed out at me from his eyes, such a chilling glare that stabbed at me from in there. The feeling was utterly creepy and unearthly. I looked into the eyes of the person I had known, that up until recently had been so warm, friendly and smiling, and found that something, or more precisely someone, totally unfamiliar and infinitely hostile was looking back at me through those eyes, spurting out deathly cold and deadly malevolence. For an instant I was literally petrified; I simply couldn't move. At home, weeping and praying, I gradually came to terms with the terror I had experienced and understood that this wasn't his hatred. It was not at all a human hatred. I had stood before the gaze of Satan himself.

In the same way, from behind the human gaze of the comforters, which at first glance seems friendly, sympathetic and compassionate, but in reality is distorted and destructive, at times icily searing both Job and the reader, we see the terrifying un-human glare of the one who is essentially directing this distortion and condemnation, and who sees in this destructiveness the seal of his victory. The Accuser began by

---

[64] Mark 13:22

trying to slander Job before God, but he who comes in order *to steal, and to kill, and to destroy*[65] was finally satisfied by succeeding in slandering Job in front of his friends.

A witness in heaven

One of the earliest texts of the *Tenach,* it seems as if the Book of Job was inspired by God as a type of preface to our history, the history of the **chosen people**. The same principles function in our history except that whereas in the Book of Job we see the private tragedy of one man, in the history of a people placed by God in the center of His plan, it turns into a tragedy for all mankind. Our Adversary is extremely interested in making the distance between Israel and Gentile believers in Jesus seem insurmountable, in this way ensuring that God's plan appears impossible to attain. I wholeheartedly believe that this is the reason the Lord has prompted me to begin our discussion about the suffering of Israel and the place of Israel in God's plan from this particular point.

Through the story of Job, of which you and I are the readers and observers, the Lord is teaching believers what the players in the grander scheme must know and see – both those in the role of Job, and those in the role of his friends. Perhaps it is not our favorite pastime these days to examine the judgmental and merciless comforters of Job, who from within his story couldn't, or didn't want to, correctly interpret his suffering and see the situation from God's perspective. It is specifically in looking at them, however, that I sense all the more emphatically the command and leading of the Lord to protect Israel from *worthless physicians*[66] and to offer another, non-traditional (could it possibly be God's?) perspective on the suffering of Israel. I so identify with the heart-cry of Job, who knew that no one but God Himself could defend him and would stand up for him. *'Now put*

---

[65] John 10:10
[66] Job 13:4

down a pledge for me with Yourself. Who is he who will shake hands with me?'[67]

That light, that *width and length and depth and height*[68] of God's love at which the heart of Job bursts open from within the seemingly impenetrable darkness of his suffering, invariably startles and stirs the heart. Even while resenting God for striking him, in the depth of his being Job knows that God Himself is his only intercessor, the sole witness who will help him stand before the people condemning and hurling abuse at him. *'Surely even now my witness is in heaven, and my evidence is on high.'*[69] It is difficult to find words more fitting for a transition from the distress of Job to the distress of Israel. The faithfulness of God to His people seen against the backdrop of mankind's treachery and hatred is the regularly resounding motif of the *Tenach,* which always has been and to this day remains the legacy of our earthly history. *'If it had not been the LORD who was on our side,'* let *Israel now say – 'If it had not been the LORD who was on our side, when men rose up against us...'*[70] Just like Job, we also know (and if earlier we knew it only theoretically, then from the time of the so-called Al-Aksa intifada it has become a tangible daily reality) that in all the world there is no one to vouch for us apart from God. There is no one besides Him and His words, whom I could call upon to protect Israel. Today, similar to how Job does from the pages of his story, I cry out to the Living God from the pages of the story in which you and I are now players, entreating His protection and intercession. For who else will stand up for us?

A special place in God's plan

When speaking to the newly converted Gentiles centuries after Job, the Apostle Paul alerted them to God's eternal love for Israel

---

[67] Job 17:3
[68] Eph. 3:18
[69] Job 16:19
[70] Ps. 124:1-2

and urged them not to *be haughty, but fear.*[71] Similarly, with our bird's eye view of Job's story you and I could tell his comforters the same thing: Don't be haughty! Don't *be wise in your own opinion.*[72] Just because Job has been struck with all imaginable disasters, this does not necessarily mean that he has been discarded by God and that the coveted place of God's chosen one is now vacant. In the last chapter Job's comforter-friends find out for themselves that God still loves Job and has not left him, but until that last chapter arrives the temptation to judge Job (and think oneself wise) is extraordinarily strong. It is the same with the history of Israel. For the past two thousand years, very few Gentile Christians have withstood the temptation to judge Israel and pronounce themselves as our replacement. Though today the closing stages of this earthly story are looming ever nearer, the time of that last chapter where the error of those reproving us will be made plain for all – the way the error of Job's comforters was revealed at the end of the Book of Job – is yet to come. This is why God's Word is so essential to a proper understanding of what is happening to Israel. The Book of Job does not simply shed light on our history; it is, in essence, one of God's keys to this history, unlocking it in Spirit and in truth. It is God's mirror, reflecting the path you and I are traveling, allowing us to see this path through God's eyes and to understand how frighteningly immense the discrepancy is between His heavenly plans and their human interpretations on the ground.

The comforters that came to visit Job perceived the hand of God in his sufferings and condemned him based on this. The "heavenly prologue" leaves us with no doubt that God is indeed allowing these sufferings; however, it is crucial that we understand (and this is one of the main lessons of the Book of Job, by no means intended only for his comforters!) that the obviousness of this fact does not necessarily go hand in hand with sin and punishment. As we have seen, the prologue strongly affirms that the reason the Lord allowed these sufferings was not as a punishment for Job's sins. On the

---

[71] Rom. 11:20
[72] Rom. 11:25

contrary, Job was chosen because from the very beginning God loved and took notice of him: *'a blameless and upright man, one who fears God and shuns evil.'* [73] Doubtless there was sin even in Job's life, and I will be so bold as to say that though his upright, God-fearing life seemed totally submitted to God, there was an insufficiency of that very God, an inadequate honesty and vitality of relationship with the One, of whose existence Job was always aware, to whom he regularly prayed and to whom he duly brought his sacrifices. This was why the Lord needed to shake him: so at least in this way to destroy the illusion of self-sufficiency.

Having said all this, however, the story of Job is primarily a story of special election and special calling. The Author of this story purposefully makes us witnesses to the dialogue between God and Satan so that we can be convinced of the truth. God selects Job from among all inhabitants of the earth and places him in an incredibly special place. It is this special **place** in God's plan, the place to which the Lord elected and placed him, wherein Job differs from all of his prosperous, virtuous comforters; and though he is not able to understand the entirety of God's plan, he undoubtedly senses his special place: *'I also could speak as you do, if your souls were in **my soul's place.**'* [74]

Nonetheless, I am writing today not about Job, but about Israel. Job's special place in God's plan is important only as a context for our discussion ahead about the special place of the chosen people in God's plan. The history of Israel calls to memory the story of Job not only in connection with the suffering the Lord is taking us through, but even more so, our path is the path of Job primarily in connection with that special **place** in the plan of God to which, like Job, He has elected us. Israel is the son and firstborn of God, the possession of God, special, a chosen and peculiar people, separated from all others by special closeness to God. *'For what great nation is there that has God so near to it, as the LORD our God is to us, for whatever reason we may call upon Him?'* [75]

---

[73] Job 1:8; 2:3
[74] Job 16:4
[75] Deut. 4:7

Two millennia have passed since the time when all of a sudden, almost in a single hour (from the historical point of view) Israel, like Job, is transformed into a people persecuted and outcast, into something outsiders almost universally consider to have sinned against God and been abandoned by Him. Now, their pitiable distinction consists of something altogether different. *All who found them have devoured them; and their adversaries said, 'We have not offended, because they have sinned against the LORD, the habitation of justice, the LORD, the hope of their fathers.'*[76] Two thousand years into our suffering, as with the suffering of Job, people see it as the punishment of God and on this basis judge and condemn us. From the very moment when the terrible tragedy of the destruction of Jerusalem and the Second Temple struck our people, everyone began to see Israel as cast off and cursed by the Heavenly Father, one who is simply receiving the "just deserts" of infidelity and backsliding. Our countless calamities have only served to make the saints "rejoice" by proving again and again our sinfulness before God and the righteousness of God's judgment. Since that time, the seemingly endless tribulations that have been poured out on Israel are invariably declared to be God's retribution, the sign that He has rejected His people. It was not by chance that the Lord gave us the Book of Job many centuries before. Through the tragic and agonizing events recorded on the pages of the Bible, He was preparing us for just such a tragic and agonizing story of our own, saturated with real-time blood and smoke. He taught us the faith and trust of Job, who by the mercy of God overcame not only physical suffering and the sorrow of loss, but also the excruciating torture of man's accusations of being guilty before God and rejected by Him.

So it has continued from then until now, and however painful it is for me to acknowledge it (me, a Messianic Believer!), it was the coming of Yeshua to this world that designated the beginning of this path of sorrows, that activated our ascent to **that place** for which our Father has chosen us, and to which He is leading us. Israel began their sorrowful ascent to the altar from the moment

---

[76] Jer. 50:7

Yeshua entered into His glory, and like Isaac, did not even suspect it. Yeshua rose from the dead *on the third day;*[77] His earthly mission had been completed and a new epoch was beginning. Foreshadowing this day, the Book of *Bereshit* says that *on the third day, Abraham lifted his eyes and saw the place afar off.*[78] On this *third day* the ascent began. From a distance, his gaze penetrating the centuries, seeing *the place afar off,* the Lord laid on us the *wood of the burnt offering,* took in His hand *fire and a knife,*[79] and began to lead unsuspecting Israel on their way to the altar.

The New Testament interpretation of the *Tenach* traditionally sees a symbol of the cross in this laying the wood on Isaac; interestingly enough, this same thought is echoed in the *Midrash.* "Abraham took the wood for the burnt offering and laid it on Isaac, similar to how a cross is laid on the shoulders of a person led to be crucified."[80] How could it be possible that the Jewish sages were not afraid of this comparison with a cross? The only way I can explain so pregnant a comparison, so dangerous, it would seem, from the perspective of Christian parallels and polemics, is that the true revelation of God's plan and design for Israel shines through this Biblical text, and the authenticity of this revelation outweighed all other considerations and misgivings. Isaac's path is the same one the Father is leading us down. For two thousand years Israel, accused of the murder of the Savior, continues to bear the same cross on which Yeshua was crucified – and the fire and knife never cease to accompany us, the alleged "Christ-killers", on this path of sorrows. Although the heart of the Father is bursting from agony for His son, in silence, like Abraham, He continues to lead us after Himself. *And the two of them went together.*[81]

---

[77] Acts 10:40
[78] Gen. 22:4
[79] Gen. 22:6
[80] *Midrash Raba Bereshit,* parashah 56
[81] Gen. 22:6

Together on the path

I am reminded of a story by Ilya Ehrenburg which at one time deeply stirred my heart. From the lips of his unbelieving protagonist Lasik, Ehrenburg tells a startling fable as piercing and profound as if the Lord Himself had related it to him. The setting is medieval Rome, where various forms of entertainment are invented to amuse the Pope and his priests for the festival of Shrovetide.[82] "Since the Pope loved Shrovetide, he came up with an excellent scheme: to have the Jewish community furnish a human racehorse for everyone to make sport of. On Shrovetide this unfortunate 'horse' would be forced to run around the circumference of the city stark naked, while the Pope with his bishops and ladies were to sit on golden stools and burst into the merriest peals of laughter ever heard in the city," and if he were to stop, the Pope's stablemen would immediately start to flog him with their whips.

Of course, the "racehorse" turned out to be the poorest Jewish man in the city since all others were able to buy themselves out of it, but this poor tailor had nothing save a wife and six children and didn't have anything to ransom himself with. ("Let's say his name was Laser. I think he was the grandfather of my grandfather," says Ehrenburg's narrator, a Jewish man just as poor and unfortunate, whose life consists of nothing but beatings and abuse.) When the time for the heralded race came, "the Pope crossed himself and climbed up onto his stool… and the various priests settled in around him. These were men of prayer and the Pope himself was with them, which meant that everywhere they had put up portraits of your merciful God," Lasik tells his Catholic cellmate. There were gilded golden and silver icons all around, and under these banners the "race" was to take place. The Pope rang the bell, and they brought forward the "racehorse" followed by his fearfully wailing wife and children, accompanying their father to his death. Laser bid them farewell, bid his life farewell – and ran.

---

[82] The holiday to celebrate the end of winter and coming of spring, as well as to feast before Lent, also known as Mardi Gras.

So, this doomed Jewish tailor began his last race. "The stablemen were standing everywhere. They were watching to make sure this human horse had no rest. In addition to the stablemen, ordinary people were standing around – since for whom is it not interesting to watch such two-legged horse-races? ...And all of them... shouted with laughter: 'Run, old nag!' In response, Laser would meekly answer them, 'I am running.'"

In this way, he ran around Rome once, and now barely able to lift his feet, all the more frequently the stablemen lashing him with their whips so that his whole body was bleeding, he knew that he would not have enough strength to run around Rome two more times. Still he ran, or tried to run, in order to somehow extend his miserable life just a little longer, but when he caught sight of his wife and children, and the "golden stool with the Pope sitting on it," his strength gave out. He fell to the ground and waited for death.

At that moment, all of a sudden he saw one more man running, another Jewish person. -Where did you come from? shouted the unfortunate victim. -What is your name? Get out of here! I am the one who is supposed to run and die!

-I must also run, answered the stranger. -My name is Yeshua, and I cannot rest, because they are killing in My name. I run with those who are ridiculed in My name. You have seen how they make My portraits of gold and diamonds and place them everywhere, in front of hungry children and the gallows. This Pope has invented your "merry" death, and My golden portrait hangs over him. No, I must run, I will not have peace as long as they kill My people in My name.

Then Yeshua, wanting to help and save Laser, Himself ran in his stead around Rome. The stablemen beat him, and the spectators laughed and jeered at him. When He ran all the way to the Pope, the Pope, dying of laughter, yelled at Him, "I'll show you what the Pope of Rome is! He is the authorized representative of the merciful Christ, and now straightaway you'll get a hundred lashes with the whip, so that you'll know ahead of time what it's like to crucify our God!"[83]

May this fable remain with you as an especially poignant illustration of what I am trying to say. It was not to a believer in Yeshua, but to the insightful and sincere heart of this Jewish writer that this spiritual truth was indisputably revealed. It is a truth, alas, from which many, many Christians turn away: that the terrible pain of the people of Israel, who walk this turbulent path and were chosen for persecution and suffering for their alleged rejection of the Savior, that this terrible pain belongs to Yeshua as well, Himself chosen so that His people who had ostensibly rejected Him could be burned and slaughtered in His name. It is the terrible pain of the Father carrying fire and a knife, who leads the son *(though He was a Son, yet he learned obedience by the things which He suffered[84])* with the wood on his back intended for the burnt offering that bears such a close resemblance to the cross of the One who came to be crucified. We have already asked the question, for whom was this ascent up Mount Moriah more difficult, for the father or the son? For me the pain and sorrow of the Father is the only possible answer when considering all the sufferings of my people, all the pain and sorrow of our tragic history: *the two of them went together.*[85]

A hidden warning

Paul was a man of God to whom the mysteries of God were revealed by the Spirit and expressly because of this, he did not doubt for an instant the eternal election of Israel. He addresses the Gentiles as if he had read both the prologue and the last chapter of the history of Israel, thereby knowing this history from beginning to end the way a reader of the Bible would know the story of Job. *'For I do not desire, brethren, that you should be*

---

[83] This episode was taken from Ilya Ehrenburg's narrative, "The stormy life of Lasik Roitschwantz". The text in quotation marks is a direct quote from Ehrenburg, the rest is my paraphrase.
[84] Heb. 5:8
[85] Gen. 22:8

ignorant of this mystery, lest you should be wise in your own opinion, that blindness in part has happened to Israel until the fullness of the Gentiles has come in.'[86] Unfortunately, so very few in the history of Christianity have heeded the warning of Paul not to be wise in their own eyes at the expense of Israel. Job's comforters relied on their own wisdom and godliness, and were humiliated before God for not speaking of Him *what is right*.[87] Similarly, historic Christianity, convinced that her accusations of Israel stem from her devoutness and faithfulness to God, is in reality not speaking of Him *what is right* and is distorting and perverting His Word.

In verses nine and ten of Romans eleven, Paul quotes from a Psalm: *And David says: 'Let their table become a snare and a trap, a stumbling block and a recompense to them. Let their eyes be darkened, so that they do not see, and bow down their back always.'*[88] These words are traditionally interpreted in this context to refer to the hardening of Israel, but I believe a warning to the Gentiles as well is hidden beneath their surface. The Scripture Paul is quoting here is from Psalm sixty-nine. This surprising Psalm, a Messianic Psalm prophesying the sufferings which Yeshua would undergo on the cross, among other things addresses God about the problem of *enemies*.[89] While by the Spirit of God prophesying about the Messiah's sufferings, this Psalm was originally written describing the suffering of Israel and in speaking of enemies, speaks specifically about those that persecute Israel, about those *who reproach You... who hate me without a cause,* those who *talk of the grief of those You have wounded*.[90] The words *'let their table become a snare before them, and their well-being a trap'* are for such people; it is upon them that the Psalmist asks the Lord to *pour out [His] indignation,* and to take hold of them in His *wrathful anger*.[91] In this case it is not Israel that is found to be under a curse but their enemies, the persecutors tormenting and hating them for no justifiable reason. While speaking of the hardening of Israel, Paul is adamant that

---

[86] Rom. 11:25
[87] Job 42:7
[88] Rom. 11:9-10
[89] Ps. 69:4
[90] Ps. 69: 9,4 ,26
[91] Ps. 69:22,24

the Gentiles do not gloat over them. *Do not boast,*[92] he says. Do not be *wise in your own opinion.*[93] With all their harshness, the words of the Psalm are absolutely appropriate in the Biblical context of God's enduring promise to *bless those who bless* Israel and to *curse him who curses.*[94] The Church, however, which has not heeded Paul's warning to not boast and be wise in her own eyes, similar to the comforters of Job, has not spoken of Him *what is right,*[95] and is in danger of invoking on herself all the original meaning of the curses described in Psalm sixty-nine.

The logic of the Accuser

It is evident that the original curses of this Psalm relate first and foremost to those enemies, those opponents and adversaries, possessed in countless numbers by our people. How numerous Job's were, as well, and from the depths of bitterness he protested about those who mocked him. I am eternally grateful to God for the "friends of Israel," those people truly devoted to Israel who pray for us, love us and support us, frequently despite the indifferent or hostile attitude of their own churches or congregations. Yet even among these friends, alas, there are many "comforters" who with incredible ease take it upon themselves to "diagnose" our illnesses and think they know only too well why Israel suffers. As we know, it was Job's friends that came to visit him; they were the ones who sat near him throughout the entire book, and who took upon themselves that which only God is allowed to do: to judge and convict. When in the writings of even Marzinkovsky[96] who dedicated his entire life to Israel, we find that he taught that all the sufferings of the Jewish people were caused by their spiritual deterioration, here again we must recognize this to be the "Job Comforter Syndrome" that has infected practically all of Christianity:

---

[92] Rom. 11:18
[93] Rom. 11:25
[94] Gen. 12:3
[95] Job 42:7
[96] Vladimir Marzinkovsky (1884-1971) was a Russian Evangelical preacher who in 1930 moved to 'Palestine' where for many years he led a Jewish-Arab Christian congregation.

seeing everything that has happened to Israel during the past two millennia as God's punishment. Perhaps the most important point God has given me to say in this chapter is, to be direct and to the point: dear brothers and sisters, this verdict is exactly the same before God as the unfounded conclusions of the comforters' speeches. The logic of Job's comforters or more precisely, his accusers, is the logic of the Accuser (bear in mind his title from the Book of Revelation: *the accuser of our brethren*[97]). Satan begins by trying to slander Job before God, but when he fails at this he turns into a great success in slandering Job before men: he succeeds in convincing them that the suffering of Job is the result of his spiritual failure. It is exactly the same with Israel. Satan is exceptionally persistent in slandering us before men in order to fix into the minds of Christians this "Job Comforter Syndrome", and looking at our tragic history you can see just how successful he has become. **Satan himself is the one who stands behind the traditional view of our history, which sees the sufferings of Israel during the past two millennia only as God's punishment and considers Israel to be eternally rejected by God.** The time has come for believers (at least for believers!) to finally realize that in contrast to the hardships that came upon Israel in the *Tenach* and concerning which the Lord Himself repeatedly and explicitly spoke of as punishment, Israel's tribulations following the first coming of Yeshua are not only punishment. It is time to wake up to the truth that **Israel, similar to Job, has been chosen for this special, sacrificial place** in God's plan. All that has happened to Israel since the first coming of Yeshua, just as all that happened to Job, has been for a purpose. Paul asserts that *through their fall... salvation has come to the Gentiles.*[98] Or, as the New Living Translation puts it, *His purpose was to make His salvation available to the Gentiles.*[99] Israel has fallen **for the purpose of** making it possible for the Gentiles to obtain salvation.

I would like to deliberately stipulate: I do not mean in any way to suggest that Israel has no need of repentance. It goes without

---

[97] Rev. 12:10
[98] Rom. 11:11
[99] Rom. 11:11 (NLT)

saying that my people require the experience of repentance, each Jewish person and each Israeli, just as each person on this planet requires a living, personal relationship with his Creator. It is for this that thousands upon thousands of Messianic Believers now tearfully pray. It is the link that Satan has made in minds everywhere between the spiritual condition of Israel and their suffering that must be broken. Open to that same Psalm sixty-nine we just read in connection with Paul. There, everything is laid out with absolute clarity. *'O God, You know my foolishness; and my sins are not hidden from You,'* says the Psalmist to God, while immediately adding, *'Let not those who wait for You, O Lord GOD of hosts, be ashamed because of me; let not those who seek You be confounded because of me, O God of Israel. Because **for Your sake** I have borne reproach; shame has covered my face.'*[100] For His own sake, for His purposes and His plans God has chosen and placed His people, a people whose *sins* and *foolishness*, undeniably, *are not hidden* from Him, into a uniquely special place, and all that has happened to Israel during the past two millennia is the result of this election. We have yet to speak in detail about the significance of this special place, the purpose for which the Lord is allowing the suffering of Israel, but for now it is enough that it be clearly and unequivocally heard: like Job, **Israel is not punished, but chosen** – and by asserting otherwise, not speaking of Him *what is right,*[101] you are actually rejecting God's view of the story and choosing the view of the one who resists and opposes Him.

⌘ ⌘ ⌘

Morning is coming

In the Book of Isaiah, the prophet's words powerfully characterize the time in which we live today: *He calls to me out of Seir, 'Watchman, what of the night? Watchman, what of the night?' The watchman said, 'The morning comes, and also the night.'*[102]

---

[100] Ps. 69:5-7
[101] Job 42:7
[102] Is. 21:11-12

Doubtless, this is how believers living in every era feel, and yet it seems to me that this impression of lingering and deepening night-time is being felt more intensely today than ever before. The dawn is drawing nearer, but in the meantime the darkness is growing thicker. The world is almost tangibly becoming more dim and sinister, and it is from this pre-dawn gloom that we look to His Word, as to *a light that shines in a dark place, until the day dawns and the morning star rises...* [103] The Word of God is sometimes compared to a map which a traveler consults when he finds himself in unfamiliar surroundings. When he does not have the slightest idea where he is, his success depends on how much he trusts the map and checks himself against it. This is an enormously telling comparison, and is made all the more relevant if we imagine that you have been caught by the night in a totally unfamiliar place, and in the pitch-black darkness you lean over the map with the tiniest of flashlights as your only source of light. Let us press into this light in order not to lose our way in the darkness surrounding us. Let us entrust ourselves to this map in order not to get off course or go astray. No one has ever viewed the heavenly prologue to the story of Israel, and the time of the last chapter has also not yet come, yet at the same time we have been given the prologue and epilogue of the story of Job. Let's open, then, to the last chapter of the Book of Job, where not only the prologue-conscious readers, but for the first time the direct participants of the story as well, have the opportunity to see the events of the story from God's perspective.

So here we are in Job, chapter forty-two. The plan God had for Job, like the plan that God has for Israel, is incomplete and inconceivable without this final chapter where the darkness is exchanged for light and the night for dawn. It is here that tears are turned into joy and Job is restored, and here also that Israel will be restored. For forty chapters Job was seen as rejected by God in the eyes of both friend and foe; he was almost dead in his suffering and humiliation. Now, however, we are looking at the several brief but intense lines of this last chapter that describe

---

[103] 2 Pet. 1:19

restoration, acceptance, and *life from the dead.*[104] Read it very carefully. Try to grasp the meaning of these lines because for us, those still living in *the night,* they contain the promise of what the coming morning will bring. The change Job has undergone is clearly visible from his first words spoken in this chapter, and how vast is the distance that separates the Job of this final chapter from the Job who finished his speech in chapter thirty-one, when *the words of Job [were] ended.* [105] *'I have heard of You by the hearing of the ear, but now my eye sees You,'*[106] Job says to the Lord, these simple words marking both the starting and finish-lines of that unbelievably thorny and grueling path his heart has traveled. However righteous and God-fearing our hero was at the beginning of his saga, at the end, the essence of Job's change consists of no more nor less than a renewed, resurrected, born-again heart that has come to know the living God. The error of the friends, testified to by the Lord literally in the next verse, does not imply that God did not have a work to perform in Job's heart; all his righteousness and godliness were but his point of departure, so that he would seek a living relationship with the living God. The Lord stepped forward to meet Job's challenge, answering him and revealing Himself to him, but He answered only after Job walked out his journey from the rent garments of the first chapter to the rent heart of the closing chapters.

I hardly need to explain that what we are seeing is again a part of Israel's story which has not yet come to pass. The fact that God's plan has not yet been brought to fullness on earth in no way suggests that His plan is less sure, for from His timeless perspective and in His Word, everything is already said and done. In speaking of the people others saw as struck down by God and rejected, Paul prophesies of the coming day of the restoration and resurrection of Israel in this way: *'For if their being cast away is the reconciling of the world, what will their acceptance be but life from the dead?'*[107]

---

[104] Rom. 11:15
[105] Job 31:40
[106] Job 42:5
[107] Rom. 11:15

Of all the prophecies about how the end of time will be for Israel, there is perhaps not a more expressive or striking description than the last chapters of the Book of Zechariah. We will consider these chapters, beginning with the twelfth, as one more parallel from the Scriptures, an additional map. Reading through Zechariah, one can clearly understand that as it was in the case of Job and his friends, the fact that those who condemn Israel are in error does not assume that Israel has no need for repentance. The Lord has something He wants to do in the hearts of the people of Israel, just as He had something to do in the heart of Job: the final, most wondrous chapter of our history lies ahead. '*I have **heard** of You by the hearing of the ear, but now my eye **sees** You,*' Job says to the Lord. This transition from hearing to seeing, seen so plainly in the relationship between Job and God, will be just as dramatic and true in the life of Israel. For the first time those who **heard** *the sound of the words, but saw no form; [who] only heard a voice,*[108] will *look on Me whom they pierced. Yes, they will mourn for Him,*[109] and will receive Him in tears of repentance and contrition.

Is it not oddly wonderful the way the Hebrew expresses this thought?

> *They will look **on Me** whom they pierced...*
> והביטו אלי את אשר-דקרו

While at the same time:

> *They will mourn **for Him**…*
> וספדו עליו

For me this combination of pronouns – אלי and עליו (on Me and for Him) – is one of the most vivid confirmations in the *Tenach* of the truth of our faith. Yeshua, *whom they pierced,* is one with God, the Author of these words, and therefore it says ***on Me** whom they pierced;* but they will mourn *for Him,* for Yeshua, for the One whom they saw as separate from God and whom they did not accept. It is not possible to read these prophetic words or to

---

[108] Deut. 4:12
[109] Zech. 12:10

think about this imminent meeting, about this transformation of hearts by the Spirit of God, without tears and trembling.

Comfort My people

Even as the Book of Job holds a final end for Job, it also holds one for his comforters; and although everyone has something they need to change and repent of before God, the repentance of the one does not justify the condemnation of the others. Immediately after His conversation with Job, the Lord addresses his friends, saying to them, *'My wrath is aroused against you and your two friends, for you have not spoken of Me what is right...'*[110] So it happens in the last chapter that Eliphaz, Bildad and Zophar, who up until now have had so much to say, do not utter a word. *The Lord will bring to light the hidden things of darkness.*[111] Their deception, duplicity and absence of love, their "nakedness", so to speak, was exposed in too obvious a manner for them to be able to say anything. It is here that we receive from God the utterly unequivocal confirmation of the error of those who saw punishment for sin as the reason behind Job's hardships. Undoubtedly, a great deal took place deep in Job's heart during the whole course of events, but all this was between him and God alone. Those comforters trying to fill God's shoes, out of "faithfulness to Him" condemning and judging their friend, were outright condemned by God. Regrettably, this is exactly how those who out of "faithfulness to God" condemn Israel are in fact transgressing against God.

There is no command or call in the Word of God **addressed to another people** to go and denounce Israel. Whatever the sin of Israel might be, it is before God, not before men, and only God knows how and when Israel will come to repentance and be changed. For Job, his final repentance and cleansing comes only **after** his meeting with the Lord: *'therefore I abhor myself, and repent in dust and ashes,'*[112] and this is exactly how, according to

---

[110] Job 42:7
[111] 1 Cor. 4:5
[112] Job 42:6

50

the description in Zechariah, it will take place with Israel. First the Lord reveals Himself to His people, first He pours out *the Spirit of grace and supplication,* and they *will look on the One whom they pierced,* and only afterwards *a fountain shall be opened for the house of David* unto repentance and purification *for sin and for uncleanness.*[113] Yes, Israel must go through colossal spiritual changes, but the Lord Himself and no one else will be the One to cleanse His people from their sin. *'I will remove the iniquity of that land in one day,'*[114] He promises, but until then His Word is still in effect, calling all believers to *'comfort, yes, comfort My people!' says your God.*[115]

Israel's sacrificial election

The Book of Job teaches us that "judgment based on suffering" (*'Remember now, whoever perished being innocent?'*[116]) and multiplying the sorrows of the sufferer is a grave sin in the eyes of God. It is a sin in general, and a sin that has been committed against Israel in particular. The One who judged the comforters of Job for their attitude to the suffering of Job is the same One who will also judge the nations for their attitude to the people of Israel and their suffering. This is why the last chapter of Zechariah speaks not only of Israel, but also about *the people who fought against Jerusalem.*[117] In the Book of Job the Lord accepts the sacrifice of the friends and forgives their sins only in conjunction with the prayer of Job. He sends Job the ones who condemned him so they could repent and so that Job, having repented, could intercede for them before God. *'My servant Job shall pray for you. For I will accept him, lest I deal with you according to your folly; because you have not spoken of Me what is right, as My servant Job has.'*[118]

---

[113] Zech. 12:10; 13:1
[114] Zech. 3:9
[115] Is. 40:1
[116] Job 4:7
[117] Zech. 14:12
[118] Job 42:8

The prophecy of Zechariah is absolutely parallel to this. *'And it shall come to pass that everyone who is left of all the nations which came against Jerusalem shall go up from year to year to worship the King, the LORD of hosts, and to keep the Feast of Tabernacles.'*[119] The peoples who considered Israel an outcast rejected by God, similar to the friends of Job, will discover that all this time God was closer to Israel than to any of them (as in Erhenburg's fable) and that now, if they want to be accepted and blessed by God, they must come to Israel in humility and repentance the way the comforters came to Job. Reread the last chapter of the Book of Job carefully. Go back over the last chapters of the Book of Zechariah. Perhaps the knowledge of what the end will be like will help someone understand that even today the wrath of God *is aroused against* those who do not speak of Him *what is right* by misrepresenting and denying His love for His people. Perhaps someone will awaken to the truth that already today His wrath is aroused against those who believe that God has turned away from His people. Everything that is happening to us has been foreseen by God; it is not a glitch in God's design or an oversight on His part, nor is it by any means punishment. As in the case of Job, ours is a special calling, **the Lord's special election of the one who is exceptionally dear to Him, for a unique sacrifice.** In this, and specifically in this, resides the election of Israel.

The great sacrificial significance of this election that has not yet been fully revealed either to the people of Israel themselves or to the multitudes of believing Christians who are ready to love and serve Israel – this is the substance of God's great secret. *One will say, 'I am the LORD's'; another will call himself by the name of Jacob; another will write with his hand, 'The LORD's,' and name himself by the name of Israel.*[120] The Lord gave me this word virtually immediately after I became a believer, but years had to pass before I came to understand that my double election entails not only double blessing, but also double responsibility. The Lord has laid a doubly weighty burden on us, the Messianic Believers who live in Israel: not only to carry the truth and revelation of Yeshua to our own people, but to carry forth the

---

[119] Zech. 14:16
[120] Is. 44:5

truth and revelation about Israel to our brethren in the faith as well. Because of my belief in the sacrifice of Yeshua that was revealed to me by my Heavenly Father, I will not keep silent but continually speak to my fellow countrymen about it. At the same time, I will also not keep silent about the sacrificial election of my people that was similarly revealed to me by Him, but will make my voice heard to my brothers and sisters in the faith.

In a mirror, dimly

Have you noticed how the Scripture portions chosen by the Lord for these pages have such an astonishingly common thread running through them? As in mirrors perfectly reflecting each other, doubling and tripling the image, the mystery of Israel is broken up and reflected in varying perspectives and at different angles in seemingly unrelated fragments of the Word of God. The sufferings of Job and the sacrifice of Isaac, the meditations of Paul and the prophecies of Zechariah – all these bits of Scripture, each a whole within itself, describes the spiritual inheritance of Israel. This is the reason they all harmonize with and supplement each other in such a fascinating way; in one place just one verse, in another an entire chapter, in essence speak about one and the same thing.

During my childhood, I loved to spend time at the home of my grandparents. I especially loved to go into their bedroom, carefully, on tiptoe, and creep up to the old pier-glass standing in the corner. Fascinated, I would watch as my reflection was splintered and refracted into a host of incomplete but exact images, as the leaves of the mirror reflected into each other, reproducing and multiplying me over and over. Looking at these infinite reflections, I discovered things about myself which were never seen in a regular mirror. Something similar happens on these pages: the Biblical stories collected in this book reflect each other at different angles and from diverse perspectives, returning our own reflection to us. However, only if the person looking in the mirror, as multi-faceted as it is, has a firm idea of what he originally looks like, is it possible for us to form a complete picture from all these incomplete and yet completely adequate exact mirror-like replications that we are seeing. First of all we need to form a whole, something which most people will agree that was until now *seeret* to a great extent, and belonged only *to the LORD our God*,[121] the spiritual image reflected over and over, splintered and multiplied in all these stories.

My prayer is that you would find in yourself the courage to look into this looking-glass. In the mirror-like depth of the images flowing over these pages you will see a new image, perhaps unknown to you before – but not some sort of "spiritual", "heavenly", "new" Israel, but that very Israel of the *Tenach,* the natural, actual, tangible Israel, visible only through God's eyes. The Israel, chosen and called as His own, is eternally loved by the Lord.

---

[121] Deut. 29:29

CHAPTER TWO

...and he went into his chamber and wept there.
Then he washed his face and came out; and
he restrained himself... (Gen. 43:30-31)

Where are... the yearning of Your
heart and Your mercies toward me?
Are they restrained? (Is. 63:15)

Imagine that you have just received a letter from a person very dear to you, on a subject that is of exceptionally high import for you. You have every reason to believe that the author himself is also not indifferent as to this particular subject, but he is not given to disclosing how he feels about it. The letter reads as if he is writing only about what concerns you and everything he writes is truly of great consequence to your life. Abruptly, as if a window had opened to his very heart, you come upon a few brief lines hidden in the seemingly neutral and passionless text, where the author begins to share a few words about his personal feelings, as if not able to hold back any longer. I guarantee that you will drink in these lines, reading them over and over again, soaking up every word one after another, repeatedly endeavoring to catch a glimpse of your beloved's soul.

So it is with the *Tenach.* It is so electrifying for me to discover the gems embedded in the Word of God that allow us to peek into His heart and soul, into His feelings. These spiritual portholes are not so common in the Scriptures, but each is perfectly surprising and you can pick them out from among the whole of

God's living, breathing Word by the distinctly other-worldly rhythm of their words, as well as by the accelerated beating of your own heart. Oh, how I love these irrational Bible stories that seem to defy all logic! I, like the majority of people on this planet, possess a logical frame of mind – and this is why my heart pounds so fiercely when it senses the advancing of another way of thinking, the approach of other laws. It happens to all of us when we draw near to our own *Peniel*, where we see Him if perhaps not *face to face*,[122] then at least from a somehow closer vantage point and in a different light. Unquestionably, the whole Bible is the Word of God, it is His revelation – but His revelation about us is one thing, and these fleeting moments of His revelation about Himself are quite another. God's "psychology", if you will, is revealed to us through such places in the Scriptures not only to simply shake us emotionally, but taking hold of the revelation of His heart is crucial to every sort of conversation or meditation in which the believer finds himself. For those who love the Almighty God, could there be arguments more weighty or convincing than His tears and His joy?

The story of Joseph and his brothers is one such segment of the Scriptures where He invites us to look into His soul. This gripping and passionate Bible story sheds a ray of light onto the character of God and allows us to brush up against the great mystery of His love. Just as in "real life", so long as the tale continues there is much sin, brutality and injustice, much pain and many tears, but finally the moment comes when all of this ugliness is inundated and ignited with such light, such joy and love, that you involuntarily stagger backwards, not able to bear the shining brightness, your hand shielding your eyes from the blinding light. It is then that the heart all but weeps from happiness, as if experiencing a foretaste of that promise which becomes all the more precious with each day of this earthly existence, each passing year with its successive moments of sorrow, crying and pain. This is the pledge on which your hope depends: *and God will wipe away every tear from their eyes; there*

---

[122] Gen. 32:30

shall be no more... sorrow, nor crying. There shall be no more pain, for the former things have passed away.[123]

I would draw our attention to three levels, or layers, in this story. The first most external layer is **the brothers and Joseph** and all that takes place between them (and between the brothers and God). By this time we have read all the way to Genesis chapter forty-two. The day has finally come, the long-awaited moment has arrived when Joseph's brothers come to Egypt and stand before him – the ten brothers who had nearly murdered him but took enough pity on him as to sell him into slavery instead. *So Joseph recognized his brothers, but they did not recognize him.*[124] From this moment begins either a game of cat-and-mouse, or perhaps hot-and-cold; something starts to take place that is not quite visible from our outsiders' vantage point because similar to the Book of Job, the main story-line is being played out within the participants' hearts. Beginning from that moment, it is as if an invisible hand were stealthily creeping closer to that deep, dark and forbidden thing the brothers had concealed all these years not only from others, but from themselves as well. Each scene, each step taken in this story fills their hearts with progressively greater confusion and fright; with each succeeding event, they feel the invisible hand getting "warmer", slowly but surely nearing that secret, buried spot in their hearts. Although the path traveled by the Spirit of God within a human heart is deliberately obscured so that we cannot trace it perfectly, we will attempt to outline at least the major milestones of His passing.

Secrets of the heart

When Joseph's brothers arrive in Egypt, we read that Joseph *spoke roughly to them,* accusing them of being spies and of coming *to see the nakedness of the land.*[125] To be "intellectually honest", we must admit that this accusation as well as what follows it is devoid of normal logic, and there is no rational explanation for

---

[123] Rev. 21:4
[124] Gen. 42:8
[125] Gen. 2:7,12

what we are witnessing. In this sense, their entire dialogue strongly calls to mind God's conversation with Job in the final chapters of the Book of Job, or in fact God's dialogue with any of us. What He speaks to your heart is only vaguely comprehensible to others, not being intended for them, while at the same time His words are full of meaning for you. At first glance, all that Joseph says lacks any hint of comprehensibility. Why does he accuse them of spying all of a sudden? Why does he say to them, *in this manner you shall be tested,* and this is how it will be seen *whether there is any truth in you:*[126] bring your brother that is presently not with you? If he is already accusing them, then what could be the connection between the brother left at home and the accusation leveled against them? On the other hand, are you aware of what happens inside your heart when the voice of God has caught up with you? Suddenly the most inner, sensitive part of you, for long years hidden away and purposely concealed from Him, is ripped open. As unexpected as this accusation might have sounded to them with its subsequent demand to fetch their younger brother, despite its lack of sense and the total absence of a plausible connection with the accusation itself, it did not appear unreasonable to them. *Then they said to one another, 'We are truly guilty concerning our brother, for we saw the anguish of his soul when he pleaded with us, and we would not hear; therefore this distress has come upon us.'*[127] Note that God is not yet mentioned here – they have yet to understand that none other than the Almighty Himself has made them participants in this game. We still hear impersonal and passive verb forms: *this distress has come upon us,* and *his blood is now required of us (נדרש דמו);*[128] they still credit what is happening to the whims and ruthlessness of the Egyptian governor and consequently, to nothing more than an unlucky turn of events, and yet... in their deep inner recesses, a curious **spiritual** connection between what is happening to them and that long-ago story is already beginning to be revealed to them. Through the apparently irrational and inconsistent visible circumstances, another invisible logic begins to make its way to the surface – the

---

126 Gen. 42:15,16
127 Gen. 42:21
128 Gen. 42:22

logic of the movement of God's Spirit in the heart of the person He is pursuing.

In a book dedicated to God's love for His people, it was not my intention to broach the subject of Israel's guilt or repentance, but such is the nature of a reflection. Upon casting a near-accidental glance into the depths of the mirror, suddenly you notice something that comes as a complete surprise and you are unexpectedly caught off-guard. So it is that God's revelation inevitably reveals much more than you originally imagined it could. Each person who has ever had such an experience knows how multi-dimensioned the truth of God is, and the impossibility of compressing it into a standard format that can be fully comprehended by man. Try placing a three-dimensional figure on a flat surface: lumpy and bulging, it will never be able to shed the additional dimension you wish it to discard. The analogy is of course limited, since it is impossible to compare a revelation of the living God to a lifeless geometric figure, and yet it gives us a glimpse of that "additional" dimension which is necessarily present when comparing the things of God with the things of men. It gives us a sense of the multi-dimensional character of God's truths, which are only able to be confined to the two-dimensional plane of man's understanding in a way that makes them devoid of their original volume.

Perhaps this is why, in describing the brothers standing before Joseph and what is happening in their hearts as a result of the working of God's Spirit, I simply cannot but be reminded of my people. I cannot refrain from speaking out about how something so very similar is happening with us too, when not only the religious wince at the bare mention of the name of Yeshua, but even the most secular Jewish people as well. It is well-known that in religious traditions, rejection of Christianity and Yeshua is instilled literally alongside mother's milk, and so in this case the enmity is almost instinctive. It strikes me as especially ironic, however, that even secular Israelis, who in their persistence to *be like all the nations*[129] are enamored by everything under the sun from yoga to Marxism and yet do not see anything wrong with

---

[129] 1 Sam. 8:5

this, no betrayal of their Jewish identity – even they get incredibly tense around anything that involves Yeshua.

Take even the tiny Israeli plus-sign, forlornly different from all other plus-signs in the world due to its shortened stem,[130] and even it carries in itself the overt negatively-charged revulsion and rejection. With each appearance of what should have been a harmless mathematical symbol without any further semantic burden, our misshapen plus-sign does all it can to remind us that even it has nothing to do with Yeshua, nor anything to do with His cross. Paradoxically, as is always the case, this little unfinished plus-sign reminds me of Yeshua and His cross every time I look through my children's textbooks or homework, and I can speculate that I am not the only one who sees the cross through all these rigorous attempts to emphasize the absence of any connection to it. Yes, we endeavor with everything within us to keep ourselves from touching that closely guarded, centuries-old sore spot that is associated with the name of Yeshua. It is true that for nearly every Jewish person, the cross is a torturous reminder of centuries of suffering and humiliation, yet somewhere in the depths of our being we know that it is at this spot where we will eventually be overtaken, that this story is not over for us, and that a meeting with Yeshua yet awaits us. We are exactly like the brothers who sense the imminent approach of this future Meeting, who are cognizant that Someone invisible is coming closer and closer to that forbidden spot which up until then they had determined never to open up to anyone. And though they would never have acknowledged it even to each other, they know upon returning home that this story simply can not go unfinished.

A brush with the living God

The brothers set out on their way back, a journey that passes almost without incident – almost, that is, if you don't consider

---

[130] The mathematical plus-sign in Israel looks like an inverted T, with the vertical line appearing only above the horizontal line, not below it, to avoid any similarities with a cross.

the fact that while stopping for the night one of them notices the silver he had used to pay for the grain returned in his sack. *Then their hearts failed them and they were afraid, saying to one another, 'What is this that God has done to us?'*[131] They still do not realize that this story is much bigger than a trip to buy grain, that it is not about silver but about the brothers themselves – and that not their gifts are sought after, but their hearts. At the same time, the enigmatic circumstances fill them with confusion and fear as they gradually begin to understand that everything happening to them is not simply a twist of fate, but *God has done* it to them. I cannot fail to mention that such a break with the usual state of affairs as we see here, this sudden change of handwriting on the face of what had been normal life, is almost always a sure sign that the hand of God is at work – and although this, of course, is by no means His only method to get us to look at Him, these disturbances in the usual, rational pattern of things do a good job of shaking us.

One of my most vivid brushes with God before I became a believer was a dream where, in my dream, I walked into my room and somehow sensed in the core of my being that **something was not right** (I literally felt my hair bristling at that moment). Not able to figure it out and looking around the room, I tried to identify the reason for my fear, until suddenly I understood with perfect, piercing clarity: the cord of the T.V. was not plugged into the wall, and yet **the television was on.** I cannot express how terrifying this was for me and I don't know why God should be revealed to me in this way, since I was almost indifferent to the television set and hardly ever turned it on. What I do know is that I, yet an unbeliever, for the first time not so much as understood as felt absolutely and unmistakably that there was Someone who had allowed me to exist up until then according to the laws of this world, but for whom it would be nothing to remove all these laws and all this logic in one blink of an eye. This unwillingness of His – whenever He doesn't fancy it – to constrain Himself to natural laws and limit Himself to the usual, logical way of things, gave me quite a shock back

---

[131] Gen. 42:28

then. It was likely that the brothers were similarly scared when upon returning home, they all found their silver in the mouths of their sacks. In contrast to me at the time of my dream, they believed in God; yet for many years they had run from Him and hidden from His sight that dreadful sin of which they had not yet truly repented, and when such an inexplicable, irrational adventure interrupted their lives they became very frightened. After all, they had simply gone down to Egypt to buy grain (just as many centuries later the Samaritan woman had simply gone to the well for water), and they least of all expected – and least of all wanted – an unusual confrontation on this trip. What now were these uncanny things happening to them? Like a doubly-exposed roll of film with its images overlapped, we can see God's as of yet invisible reality placed over their routine lives and beginning to show through. Yes, they brought the grain home and the silver they paid for it somehow came back along with it, but something else besides this and thoughts of the brother left captive in Egypt does not let them rest. The peculiar taste of the current situation is somehow associated in their hearts with that other long-ago story, which all these years had fettered the ten of them together into a brooding and bitter union. Although at first Jacob emphatically refuses to permit Benjamin to go back with them, as if closing the issue altogether, I think that in their hearts the ten knew that this story would be obliged to continue.

The second journey begins

Guaranteeing the safe return of Benjamin, the brothers – first Reuben, then Judah – beg their father to let him go with them. Together with Benjamin they return to Egypt, filled with expectations of gloom and doom. They were apprehensive of being accused of stealing the silver they had found in their sacks; they didn't know whether they would find Simeon alive and whether he would be returned to them; and most of all they were afraid that Benjamin, upon whose coming the Egyptian magistrate had insisted, would for some reason be taken from them. When upon Joseph's order they are brought to his house, *now the men were afraid because they were brought into Joseph's house; and they said, 'It is because of the money, which was returned in our sacks the first time, that we are brought in, so that he may make a case against us and seize us, to take us as slaves with our donkeys.'*[132] But the steward of Joseph's house to whom they tried to return the silver answered them, *'Peace be with you, do not be afraid. Your God and the God of your father has given you treasure in your sacks...'* *Then he brought Simeon out to them.*[133] So, contrary to their expectations, everything began to turn out not so badly after all, and it got even better after once again they – now with Benjamin – came and stood before Joseph. He not only spoke with them in a rather softer and friendlier tone than the previous time, but also invited them to a joint meal, where the brothers were seated in order, *the firstborn according to his birthright and the youngest according to his youth* – and once again they got the impression that somebody present knew them and was aware of their secrets – *and the men looked in astonishment at one another.*[134]

As soon as the morning dawned, the men were sent away, they and their donkeys.[135] For some reason it seems to me that the dawn must have been gray and overcast that morning, and that the day promised to be dark and foreboding, but I think that the hearts of the brothers, having set off on their way back home, were filled with such jubilation that they didn't need the sun to shine. Everything had come to an end surprisingly without mishap: all the brothers – including Simeon and Benjamin – were returning home, sacks full of grain; moreover, that stern Egyptian governor had suddenly befriended them and even invited them for a feast. In his novel, Thomas Mann writes that Benjamin, sensing some undisclosed secret left behind them, did not want to leave; perhaps it did happen this way, so distinctly was God's handwriting displayed on the whole chain of events that the perceptive heart could not but feel it, but in any case the Scriptures are silent on this count. We know that at dawn they were sent away and started back on the road, but we also know

---

[132] Gen. 43:18
[133] Gen 43:23
[134] Gen. 43:33
[135] Gen. 44:3

that not long before they had left, Joseph had commanded his steward (to his great puzzlement, I imagine, as well as to the puzzlement of those reading these chapters for the first time) to put his – Joseph's – silver cup into Benjamin's sack. Next we read: *When they had gone out of the city, and were not yet far off, Joseph said to his steward, "Get up, follow the men; and when you overtake them, say to them, 'Why have you repaid evil for good? Is not this the one from which my lord drinks, and with which he indeed practices divination? You have done evil in so doing.'" So he overtook them, and he spoke to them these same words.*[136]

Stop here. Try to imagine what the eleven must have been experiencing, already anticipating the reunion with their father and their families, with stories told not without a little bragging about how they had unexpectedly become friends with the chief Egyptian governor. Already sure that everything had gone so smoothly and expediently, they were rejoicing in the uncommonly good nature of this capricious lord when his hand, which had allowed them to get but a few steps away, once again overtook them. What would they have felt when, already imagining themselves to be free, in the end it turned out that this was only a continuation of that same on-going game of cat-and-mouse from their first meeting? *So he searched. He began with the oldest and left off with the youngest.*[137] I can almost see them before me in these moments during the search: panting and crimson, trying to come to terms with yet another unforeseen misadventure, indignant with the total injustice and groundlessness of the new accusation. *'Look, we brought back to you from the land of Canaan the money which we found in the mouth of our sacks. How then could we steal silver or gold from your lord's house?'*[138] Despite all this, however, while being absolutely sure of themselves and each other, presenting their sacks to the servant of this Egyptian governor who won't leave them alone, their utterly distraught hearts are filled to the brim with mixed feelings of puzzlement, fear, affront and triumph over each one's innocence proven. Now everything is almost over, just one more

---

[136] Gen. 44:4-6
[137] Gen 44:12
[138] Gen. 44:8

moment and at last they will be released and can get moving on their way home again, far away from this strange place where evidently something mysterious was at work, far away from this sinister person who for some reason causes their hearts to shudder in remembrance of that long ago perpetrated act. Just one more minute, only Benjamin's sack is left to be checked and he of course is the youngest, the most pure among them, innocent of even what all of them are guilty of. How could he even be suspected of anything? Is there even any need to search his bag at all? Dancing around nervously with impatience, each brother has already loaded up his donkey. They are just about ready to get back on their way – hurry, come on, let's get going... hey, what's going on? What?!! I hear a moan of terror multiplied ten times over at the end of verse twelve: *the cup was found in Benjamin's sack,* and only Benjamin is left speechless and doesn't say a word.

Benjamin

This is a critical point in our account because here for the first time it becomes clear what, or more precisely whom, the whole business is about. Take another look and you will see a swift, discernible reshuffling on the stage: instead of eleven brothers exiting Egypt in one solid, massive group, we now see a group of ten, clearly and visibly congealing – adjacent the one. The one, who up until now has said and done the least, who was a participant neither in the crime of the brothers nor in their first meeting with Joseph, the one from whose lips we literally hear not a single word in all the Scriptures – this is the one who completely without warning now winds up being the central character of our plot. It is as if the outer crust of the narrative crumbles, revealing the next interior layer, the deeper second level of our story – **the brothers and Benjamin.**

Similar to the Book of Job, we the readers are shown details kept from those actually participating in the story. In contrast to them, you and I know that none other than Joseph himself is the author of the set-up with the cup, and therefore the culprit directly responsible for the current suffering of Benjamin. Why would Joseph want to do such a thing? Why does he purposefully condemn his beloved brother to this trial? If Joseph wanted to find out whether or not his brothers had repented of what they had done to him, then clearly at the end of their first meeting they had already said to each other, *'We are truly guilty concerning our brother, for we saw the anguish of his soul when he pleaded with us, and we would not hear; therefore this distress has come upon us.'*[139] We remember that having heard this (they didn't know, of course, that he was listening or could understand their conversation), Joseph *turned himself away from them and wept.*[140] I think that from the point of view of Joseph's relationship with his brothers, at this moment everything had already made an about-face. As far as the brothers went, they had repented of their sin concerning Joseph; as for Joseph, he had forgiven their sin against him – so the first meeting, in this sense, was fully sufficient. What in the world could be so important for him as to delay their reconciliation any further? And what did poor Benjamin have to do with it? Benjamin did not have any part in Joseph's sale by the other brothers and knew nothing of it; Benjamin was his own, full-blood brother who together with his father would have agonizingly and extensively mourned his death; what would seem more natural than, having revealed himself to his repentant brothers, requesting that they quickly bring Benjamin and their father so he could hold them in his arms at last? Why was it necessary to keep up this charade, but this time involving his innocent younger brother in it? Why was it necessary to frame this beloved brother and accuse him, of all people, of stealing?

Together we will attempt to answer this question. For many years Joseph, knowing nothing of his family, also could not have known anything about how things between his brothers and Benjamin were all this time. He could likely guess that they held no special love for his younger brother. Made all the more embittered as a result of their criminal act and the inconsolable sorrow of their father, in all probability upon their return home

---

[139] Gen. 42:21
[140] Gen. 42:24

the brothers vented their wrath and hard-heartedness on the one most directly related to the dreamer who had "forced" them to commit such a terrible transgression. He could assume that all these years Benjamin had unknowingly borne the brunt of their sin and had been weighed down under this burden. Yes, Joseph could speculate not a little, so well did he know his brothers, having personally experienced their rage and resentment – but he wanted to know for sure. While forgiving them their envy, which at one time they had been guilty of before him, he wanted to find out whether their hearts were now filled with the same feelings toward his younger brother. This is the reason he decided to test his brothers with Benjamin as the bait. This is why when sitting together for the meal, *Benjamin's serving was five times as much as any of theirs.*[141] Joseph, sitting separately as he was yet in the same room and covertly listening to everything being said, could easily tell whether they were envious and angry or whether they would rejoice in the uncommon favor of the Egyptian magistrate towards their younger brother. This is why it was into Benjamin's sack Joseph chose to place the cup. Naturally it was not Benjamin, whose innocence no one doubted, who was being tested with this false accusation, but his ten brothers.

Was not Joseph taking a risk with Benjamin? Imagine this group of ten as they, violence on their strained faces, breathing heavily and wielding clenched fists, stand opposite Benjamin. Who could be sure how the ten might react? At one point they had nearly torn his older brother to pieces – what would they now do to the younger, whose fault it was a second time of bursting their dream bubble of returning home, which had seemed all but realized just minutes ago? Perhaps there were those among them who from the beginning did not doubt Benjamin's innocence, but I am convinced that there were also those who were more than ready to beat him up then and there. I would suppose that Joseph had given the necessary order to his guards should this happen, but even if he had taken care that Benjamin would escape whole and physically unharmed from this situation, in

---

[141] Gen. 43:34

any case the mental and spiritual ordeal to which he had subjected his younger brother was by no means a walk in the park. The accusation of stealing was a terrible charge for a believer in the living God of Israel. *Then they tore their clothes, and each man loaded his donkey and returned to the city.*[142] What must Benjamin have felt during the somber ride back? He was innocent – and knew that God knew the same; but the cup had been found in his bag and this meant that in the eyes of his brothers as well as in the eyes of the Egyptian (so he thought), he was a thief. Of whether his brothers railed against him or remained silent, whether they were prepared to believe his innocence despite what they had seen with their own eyes or whether they didn't trust him – we know nothing, but I believe he kept silent, not wanting to justify himself before man: not before the Egyptians, nor before his brothers. He remained outwardly quiet and only his heart, his believing heart which from childhood had been taught to trust, pray, and seek God's intercession, noiselessly cried out, "God, where are You? Why are You letting this happen? But You know that I am innocent! *'Why have You forsaken Me?'*[143] Why do you `remain silent, why do you not intervene, why do you not protect and stand up for me?"

Laban's search revisited

Ashamed, crushed and confused, not having the slightest idea of what great joy lay ahead at the end of this path, what was going through Benjamin's thoughts? What memories were evoked, what did he feel during this cheerless return to the city? Did he remember what you and I will now recall, the chronicle of the idols stolen by his mother Rachel when Jacob fled Laban, with Laban's search immediately following? Though we can't be sure how closely the text of our chapter thirty-one of *Bereshit* approximates the story Benjamin would have heard as a child, told and retold by the lips of Jacob, let's turn there now. After

[142] Gen. 44:13
[143] Ps. 22:1

long years of serving Laban, Jacob decides to return to his land; or to be more accurate, God made the decision and Jacob was obedient to His will. I must qualify this statement, however. As often happens with believers, in carrying out the will of God and thus justifying his actions, Jacob did not fulfill God's will in such a godly manner. He broke off his relationship with Laban and left in a rather ungodly fashion. His whole departure or flight, rather, was so unseemly that the Word of God accuses both Jacob and Rachel of the hideous sin of theft. Not only Rachel stole, or *had stolen* (ותגנב רחל) *the household idols that were her father's*, as everybody remembers, but to our great surprise we discover that Jacob *stole away*, or "stole the heart of Laban" (ויגנב יעקב את-לב לבן),[144] because he did not inform him that he was leaving and taking with him all his wives and children, i.e. Laban's daughters and grandchildren. So Jacob leaves, but after some time Laban overtakes him and accuses him of both the fact that he had run away, as well as of stealing his idols. Jacob, indignant at the accusation and not knowing of his wife's theft, offers Laban to search the whole camp. *'With whomever you find your gods, do not let him live.'*[145] And Laban commences his search.

If you have ever read children's magazines to your young ones, you are sure to have seen exercises in comparison: either you must find the difference between two nearly identical pictures or vice versa, locate the common things hidden in two not-so-similar pictures, such as matching details virtually inconspicuous due to their more obvious differences. These two stories of searching can serve as a model for both cases. While generally similar, these two scenes have plenty of differing external details; despite all these surface differences, however, there is an inner unity not immediately observable that makes these stories spiritual twins. Remember that Jacob, overtaken and accused by Laban, is absolutely convinced that as a matter of principle there couldn't be any stolen goods in his camp, and to the depths of his being he is insulted by such suspicion. With his reverence for God, Jacob knew well that stealing was sin, and even the thought that he might somehow be mixed up in theft

---

[144] Gen. 31:19-20; in the Hebrew the word "steal" is used twice in a row practically.
[145] Gen. 31:32

was unbearable to him. Despite all this, however, he was not aware that he had sinned against Laban. He did not sense that to "steal a heart", or to deceive, was also theft, also a sin. For me this is a sure sign that he did not yet possess a vital relationship with the living God, without which it is impossible to grasp such a concept. In exactly the same way, the insulted brothers who have been accused of stealing by the steward of Joseph's house swear to their innocence in literally these same words: *'With whomever of your servants it is found, let him die.'*[146] Just like Jacob, however, they do not realize they are guilty of sin before Benjamin. They do not consider their same invisible "stealing of a heart", jealousy, extreme dislike and guile, to be sin. For me, this again points to one thing: the brothers do not yet have the type of living relationship with God where the religious heart, illuminated for the first time by the Spirit of God, starts to believe and to love. Only such a heart can understand that not only is outright visible theft a sin, but the "theft of a heart", while invisible to the naked eye, is also sin. Jacob is caught by this search on the road to the Jabbock, on the way to the place he will call *Peniel,* where he sees *God face to face,*[147] on the road to the meeting that would forever change his name, character and his very life. In the same way, Joseph's brothers are still on the road to this eternally life-changing meeting. The whole scheme with the cup, and therefore all the suffering of Benjamin, was created by Joseph for the sole purpose of leading them to this meeting – but not Benjamin nor they themselves can grasp this yet.

As the story goes, Laban searches all the tents but still doesn't find his idols. Rachel had hidden and sat on them and to this day (thought Benjamin ruefully) no one had any doubts that this story had ended favorably. Certain laws exist in the spiritual world, however, that are unseen and therefore at times ignored even by believers, but nonetheless are laws just as inviolable as the law of gravity, for instance. This is why the search of Rachel, the mother who had actually stolen and yet on whom nothing was found, reverberates a generation later in as tense a drama through the search of her son, who though absolutely innocent,

---

[146] Gen. 44:9
[147] Gen 32:30

was accused of stealing, and on whom the stolen goods were found.[148]

Surely Benjamin could not help but remember Laban's search, as it reminded him all too well of what he himself had just experienced, and the peculiar spiritual symmetry of both stories could not go unnoticed by his heart. Throughout the duration of the joyless return to the city, I can see him completely immersed in his thoughts, his inner vision as if riveted to that long-ago scene, the details of which had so unexpectedly and tragically come alive for him today. Thus lost in thought, he of course does not notice (and to them, of course, it seems as if he is simply pretending not to notice) the meaningful, aggravated glares of his brothers. The tense and unusual family unity, which they had put on before their exit from Egypt as if donning clothing for travel, was now torn asunder together with the rending of their clothes. Instead of eleven before us, we once again have the ten and the one. This morning they had left the city together but paradoxically, as occurs only in God's geometry, they were destined to travel the road back on very separate paths.

A change of heart

What is happening inside the brothers on this trip back? Yes, Benjamin was once again alienated from them as he had been for all these years, but if all this time it had been their hatred that divided them, unbeknownst to him but so glaringly obvious and agonizing for them, now he was separated from them by his guilt which, I might reiterate, was called into existence solely for their sake. Have you considered the fact that Benjamin could and must be seen as guilty only in the eyes of his brothers? The Egyptians, or at least those in the story, knew just as well as you and I who had put the cup in his sack. Benjamin, for his part, could not fathom what sort of mean trick someone had decided

---

[148] This, perhaps, is one of the brightest biblical examples of the spiritual accountability that we carry not only for our children, but **to our children** as well. Each of us is obliged to remember that what he hides from God and man during his lifetime can, in the most unexpected and unpleasant way, surface in the life of his child.

to play on him, who it was and why he had put the cup there; nonetheless, he knew full well that he himself hadn't done it. Only the ten brothers did not know anything for sure. In their eyes, the brother whose innocence all these years had been a continual torment and reproach had now emerged as the only guilty one among them.

This guilt was invented to test the purity of their hearts. Such is the logic of God's refining: when He tries your heart, He won't test it with the people with whom you've never had a problem. Your willingness to allow God's love into your life will be checked purposely against the one who for many years, perhaps himself not suspecting it, has been a point of offence, who has seared and gouged your heart. This is why no matter how difficult and painful it might be for Benjamin, this story is not about him but about his brothers. We are now beholding God's conversation with them, and watching as their hearts are being wrenched inside-out under His touch. The Lord has come to them in order *to bring to light the hidden things of darkness,*[149] and those who start out on this path with rent clothing arrive at its end... with rent hearts. What He said to them we don't know, but by the end of the road these furiously scowling and glowering men, at first constantly throwing unkind glances in the direction of their younger brother riding before them, in some miraculous way have become the ones with faces red from tears, and with eyes enlightened for the first time in all these long decades. When they finally stand before Joseph, their innocence of today, which until not long ago they were ready to defend with such fury, falls away before the wave of repentance that has swept over their souls.

Greater love

So, the brothers stand before Joseph, aware perhaps for the first time with perfect articulacy that they are not so much standing before him as before God. Then Judah, tired of running from

---

[149] 1 Cor. 4:5

God and hiding it but also liberated by the decision to no longer run, says, *'What shall we say to my lord? What shall we speak? Or how shall we clear ourselves?* **God has found out the iniquity of your servants.'**[150] What a surprising declaration! It is as if truly all their lives, they had hidden their crime from God and finally, after all these games of hot-and-cold, God had *found out [their] iniquity.* He had uncovered the sin and pinned it on them. Yes, by now each one had reached the understanding that what was happening was between them and God. They had no reason and no way to justify themselves. *O Lord, righteousness belongs to You, but to us shame of face.*[151] To them the words of Joseph did not appear at all illogical. The Spirit of God, who was the One at work behind these words and in truth the Author of this whole scene, touched their hearts and Himself led the dialogue with them. This is why they accepted the unjustified accusation, the harshness of the penalty, and even the capriciousness and flippancy of the Egyptian lord with humility, as conviction and chastising from the One before whom they had long ago so terribly sinned. Even if at first, believing Benjamin to be guilty, they perhaps would have hastened to blame him, now we stand at the conclusion of God's conversation that had been churning in their hearts all this time. Everything happened exactly the way Joseph had envisioned. Only at the point when they could *lay aside the sin which so easily ensnares,*[152] the wrong attitude to their younger brother, could they become able to open their darkened hearts to the rays of God's sunlight – and only then did their full repentance and thorough cleansing also become possible. At the end of this chapter Judah says, *'Now therefore, please let your servant remain instead of the lad as a slave to my lord, and let the lad go up with his brothers.'* Judah entreats Joseph for the sake of the father, whose *life is bound up in the lad's life,* and who, *when he sees that the lad is not with them, will die;*[153] but aside from loving the brother for the sake of the father, for the first time Judah begins, in fact, to love his brother himself. *Greater love has*

---

[150] Gen. 44:16

[151] Dan. 9:7

[152] Heb. 12:1

[153] Gen. 44:30-31,33; נפשׁו קשׁורה בנפשׁו *"his soul is bound up in his soul"* (Young's Literal Translation)

no one than this, than to lay down one's life for his friends,[154] and this is the reason why Judah does exactly what Joseph had hoped for him to do.

So finally, when God's dialogue with them had come to a close, when the *fruits worthy of repentance*[155] had been brought forth, when Judah was finally ready to *lay down his life for his brother,* please note that then and only then, **Joseph could not restrain himself... And he wept aloud.**[156] Starting with the tears of Joseph, the brightest and most wonderful part of our story begins. Genesis chapter forty-five is one of the most beautiful chapters in the Bible, the chapter in which Joseph reveals himself to his brothers, in which **he fell on his brother Benjamin's neck and wept.**[157] Only then our eyes and hearts are opened to the innermost, third layer of our story, **Joseph and Benjamin.** We can now see that all these events had been so carefully planned for the sake of this brother. The attitude of the brothers towards Benjamin was so important to Joseph namely because Benjamin himself was so very precious to him. It is curious that in comparison with the usual Scriptural accounts so sparing on emotions, here the Word of God describes vividly in minute detail what is going on in Joseph's heart. It is likely that all the brothers were quite stirred when Joseph revealed himself to them, and it can be said with confidence that Benjamin's happiness knew no bounds, but we find almost nothing about this in our text, save for a scant mention that Benjamin also *wept on his neck.*[33] Judging by these facts, the Lord must have deemed it very important to communicate to us how great was the joy of Joseph in particular, having regained his brothers and most notably, having recovered Benjamin. And, if it is so important for Him to have paid special attention to this detail, then it is important that you and I hear it.

❋ ❋ ❋

[154] John 15:13
[155] Mat. 3:8
[156] Gen. 45:1-2
[157] Gen. 45:14

The unseen reality

Why? Why is it so important for us, someone might ask? Yes, it's a nice story, only why is it here in this book? Needless to say, I am by no means the first to whom the Spirit of God has revealed that this meeting in Genesis chapter forty-five between Joseph and Benjamin is a type of the meeting we all long for, the meeting we previously read about in the prophet Zechariah: *then they will look on Me whom they pierced.*[158] This is the meeting for which we are in constant prayer, the meeting of Yeshua and Israel. Yet, if we follow the logic of God's revelation, then Joseph as the image of Yeshua gives us surprising insight not only into His plan, aiding us in our appreciation for Israel's role in this plan, but also into the soul, the heart, the sentiments of the Lord. It allows us to "eavesdrop" on His feelings regarding Israel. At the beginning of this chapter we spoke of a letter, the author of which had opened his heart a crack, so to speak, in just a few short lines. In the story of Joseph and his brothers, it is as if God had folded back the shutters to the windows encasing that very *chamber*, or "inner room", where He desires to unveil His heart to us. With this remarkable story, the Lord is teaching us to see His true self, teaching us to discern the difference between what He is feeling and what He might be doing, even though His actions seem to contradict His feelings at times. He wants for us to learn that what is true and real is often not visible, and that to "see" this unseen truth based on our natural vision is practically impossible. *Now faith is the substance of things hoped for, the evidence of things not seen.*[159] This is the faith we must endeavor to attain.

Let us return to our story, but a day or two prior to where we left off. Remember how in Genesis chapter forty-three the brothers, having traveled to Egypt together with Benjamin, now stand before Joseph? Take a look at this scene: stomachs knotted from the stress of their dim expectations (though putting all their efforts into appearing sociable and agreeable) the brothers uncomfortably shift from one foot to the other, frowningly

---

[158] Zech. 12:10
[159] Heb. 11:1

studying this strange face awash with "Egyptian aloofness" (I think they may have seen it this way), trying to guess what awaited them this time. Ten of them had already been here before and this whole scene was an unpleasant *déjà vu* for them. Worn out from the uncustomary dependence, they looked forward with agonizing impatience to the finale. Only Benjamin, laying eyes for the first time on the one about whom he had heard so much, with open curiosity examines this strange man. Who is he? Why has he been so insistent on his, Benjamin's, coming? And what is even more peculiar, now that Benjamin has finally come, why does he not even bother to look at him?

Have you noticed this point that must have amazed Benjamin so much? From the moment the brothers come before Joseph and he begins to speak with them, until the moment *he lifted his eyes and saw his brother Benjamin, his mother's son,*[160] an entire eternity passes. Four verses of Scripture can make up several very long moments in real life. Could it possibly be that Joseph really did not notice Benjamin until now? The astute heart understands, however, how much these long, drawn-out minutes mean. This single dramatic detail is enough to show how infinite is the love Joseph has for his brother. Who among us has not at least once, maybe in childhood, experienced something similar? When someone or something, the object of your tireless expectations and dreams, is finally before you, having so passionately and for so long dreamt about this instant, you are now afraid to lift your eyes in that direction for fear that the mirage might dissolve, or that you will be overwhelmed and your heart explode, afraid lest it all turn out to be a dream... or lest you rush too quickly headlong into the swelling tides of limitless mind-boggling happiness which now threaten to engulf you in their power. Joseph, who doubtless had noticed Benjamin from the second he entered, continues to converse with the others as if unaware of the newcomer. With all his might he refrains from looking over at that brother before the right time comes, because he recognizes that when he does he will no longer be able to speak, unable to resist being swept away on the wave of emotions that

---

[160] Gen. 43:29

overpower him. Only after all the obligatory words of welcome are pronounced does he allow himself this indulgence. He permits himself for the first time to look fully upon *his mother's son*. He allows himself to *lift his eyes and see his brother Benjamin*[36] and to look, forgetting everything and everyone, absorbing these infinitely dear features… until they become suspiciously foggy, until they begin to swim about and his eyes burn with something unbecoming and impermissible, something indecently warm and salty. *Now his heart yearned for his brother; so Joseph… sought somewhere to weep.*[161] The description of Joseph's feelings is acutely intense in the Hebrew:

Now his heart yearned for his brother
כי-נכמרו רחמיו אל-אחיו

This is one of the strongest, if not the strongest, expressions in the *Tenach* to describe the feelings which permeate a loving person. When King Solomon, for example, was determining the mother of the infant and made as if to have the child divided in two with the sword, it is said of the real mother:

She yearned with compassion for her son [162]
נכמרו רחמיה אל-בניה

This same phrase is used several times in the *Tenach* to describe God's love for Israel: *'Therefore My heart yearns for him; I will surely have mercy on him,' says the LORD.*[163] It is intriguing that the word רחמיה/רחמיי can be translated as womb (in this sense we get the term heart, as that innermost part of us), but also as compassion, mercy, or lovingkindness. The combination of these two definitions makes that deep-down love that besieges the soul even more prominent and intense. It describes the emotion with which Joseph is overcome, like a wave swallowing him from head to foot. *Now his heart yearned for his brother; so Joseph made haste and sought somewhere to weep.*[33]

---

[161] Gen. 43:30
[162] 1 Kings 3:26; the NASB translates this phrase as, *'She was deeply stirred over her son.'*
[163] Jer. 31:20

The inner room

Now, try to see this entire scene through the eyes of the brothers. Try to imagine for yourself their puzzlement when this grim and arrogant Egyptian governor (this is probably how they would have perceived him), having already repeatedly bewildered them, unexpectedly right in the middle of their conversation, without any explanation and for no apparent reason turns and strides quickly, or all but runs, toward the exit. *So Joseph made haste.*[33] Occupied with themselves and their business, the brothers are light-years away from thoughts that could explain the reason forcing Joseph to momentarily disappear. Not one of them, including Benjamin, has the slightest idea of what is really going on in the heart of this "aloof" lord, or how *his heart yearned for his brother.*[164] *Faith is being... certain of what we do not see.*[165] It is difficult to imagine a more graphic or expressive illustration of this difference between the seen and unseen. The brothers do not see the heart-breaking scene that you and I do: *and he went into his chamber and wept there.*[33] They do not suspect what is happening with Joseph in this inner room, and for this reason the gap is truly great between how they perceive the circumstances and what is really going on in the invisible reality of that chamber.

Stop for a moment. Think back through this scene. Recall Joseph, weeping out of love in this **inner room.**[166] This is one of the central images not only of this chapter, but of our entire book. We the readers easily understand it is in *his chamber* that we see the true Joseph, and for a brief moment it might seem to us that the game is over. Now, we think hopefully, wiping his tears, Joseph will emerge from his room and rush over to Benjamin, give him a bear hug and reveal himself. I am convinced that this was exactly what Joseph wanted to do more than anything else in the world. It is perfectly **natural** to expect this from a person who finally sees a beloved brother whom he has been separated

---

[164] Gen. 43:30

[165] Heb. 11:1 (NIV)

[166] In the Hebrew, the word translated as "his chamber" from Gen. 43:30 (הַחַדְרָה), uses the definite article, indicating that Joseph probably went into a special, private room, or "inner room", as the expression of choice in our text.

from for many years. We are permitted, however, to instead come into contact with the mystery of God's love, an amazing and **supernatural** love, which holds back the tears and sends the object of love to the cross. Here we are again overtaken by that dramatic and startling apparent inconsistency between what we imagine to be love... and how His love is manifested. Joseph (revealing the character of God's love in this more than in anything else!) cannot reveal himself to the brothers until his plan is complete, until God's work in the hearts of the story's participants is finalized. For this reason, what does he do upon leaving his chamber? Completely opposite of what we might expect and what he might personally want to do, *he washed his face* so that his tears would not be seen, so that there would be no trace of that love, *and came out;* **and he restrained himself...** (*ויתאפק*).[167]

Remember this word **restrained,** remember these tears of love that Joseph had to hold back. Remember, because right from the beginning of the next chapter we are again mystified. You and I already know the whole plot, which makes it difficult to restore the initial feeling one gets when reading this story for the first time. Literally a few lines after Joseph has been overcome with tears of love for Benjamin, we read: *and he commanded the steward of his house, saying, 'Fill the men's sacks with food, as much as they can carry, and put each man's money in the mouth of his sack. Also put my cup, the silver cup, in the mouth of the sack of the youngest, and his grain money.' So he did according to the word that Joseph had spoken...*[168]

We have already discussed everything that follows: the brothers leave, the search is performed, the cup is found in Benjamin's sack. We can clearly picture the order of events which connect these two points like a dotted line. One point corresponds to what we have just read: *and he went into his chamber and wept there. Then he washed his face and came out; and he* **restrained himself...** (*ויתאפק*);[169] the other point is the story's conclusion:

---

[167] Gen. 43:31
[168] Gen. 44:1-2
[169] Gen 43:30-31

*then Joseph **could not restrain** himself... (להתאפק) and he wept aloud...*[170] From math class in school, we remember that two points can be connected by an infinite number of lines but only one of them will be straight. This is exactly what we see in our story. The two points are connected by not one but two lines. One visible, circuitous line, the view purposefully revealed to the brothers, follows the observable surface of the day's events: the *restrained* Joseph's instruction to put the cup into Benjamin's sack, the brothers' exit, the stop and the search, the return to the city, the conversation with Joseph, the speech of Judah sacrificing himself for Benjamin's sake, and finally the tears of Joseph, not restraining himself as he reveals himself to his brothers. There is a second line, however, one hidden and invisible to the natural eye but visible to us: the straight segment **directly** connecting the Joseph who weeps in secret *in the inner room* with the Joseph openly sobbing violently, who tearfully reveals himself to his brothers. The word translated into English as *restrained himself* is the Hebrew word להתאפק, meaning to hold back or control oneself. The tears of love that are held back and hidden at our first point are revealed to a full degree at the second point, when *Joseph could not restrain himself* any longer.

We become witnesses to the Author's conscientiously and purposefully built inconsistency between these two lines: between what the participants of the story see and what the reader knows and sees. Most profound of all, we discover **love** to be the secret so thoroughly hidden from the story's participants, but shown to us by the Author. In the Book of Job, we see that the Lord loved Job but until the end of the book this fact was hidden from both Job himself as well as from his judgmental comforter-friends. In our story from Genesis, Joseph loved Benjamin but again until the very end of the story, this love is hidden from Benjamin himself, and from his brothers. Only the reader who is shown the Prologue in Heaven or the tears of Joseph in *his chamber* knows without a shadow of a doubt that everything happening to both Job and Benjamin testifies to the special election and special love that has placed

---

[170] Gen. 45:1-2

them in the center of the plan. Only the reader knows that both Joseph himself and his love for his brother remain unchanged all along the invisible dotted line, and that the Joseph who causes Benjamin pain by putting the cup in his bag and accusing him of theft loves him not a fraction less than that Joseph who weeps on his neck. The only difference is that before Joseph had finished his plan with the brothers, he *restrained himself,* withholding his love for Benjamin in the same way the Lord had *restrained* and withheld His mercy until He finished His work in the heart of Job and the hearts of his comforters.

✕ ✕ ✕

From His heart to ours

The Lord has *restrained* and *withheld* His mercy? What an amazing word – **to restrain, to withhold;** what a strange expression for the Bible to use in referring to God's attitude to the one He loves! The prophet Isaiah, grieved at the wretched condition of Israel, used these words to address God. *'Where are Your zeal and Your strength, the yearning of Your heart and Your mercies toward me? Are they restrained?'*[171] Or, as another English translation expresses the Hebrew: *'Where are your zeal and your might? Your tenderness and compassion are withheld from us.'*[172] In the original Hebrew, this word translated as restrained or withheld is that same word התאפקו that we just saw used in the story of Joseph. For me the testimony of these chapters and of this word is truly priceless. As we meditate on Israel and see the relationship of Yeshua to Israel in Joseph's relationship to Benjamin, we realize that we cannot and must not judge God's intentions on the basis of visible circumstances. When for the sake of His plans He must restrain and withhold His love and mercy, the reality we see with our natural eyes scarcely corresponds to the reality of His heart, and consequently is almost always interpreted incorrectly.

---

[171] Is. 63:15
[172] Is. 63:15 (NIV)

One of the first things I was told as a new believer was that no matter what life might bring my way, God loved me and He proved it on Calvary. *Neither death nor life ... nor any other created thing, shall be able to separate us from the love of God which is in Christ Jesus our Lord.*[173] We all know these words and this principle; we all know that His ways are not our ways and that even though we don't understand everything, we are to trust Him: *...faith is the substance of things hoped for, the evidence of things not seen.*[174] When life gets uncomfortable and confusing, however, it might become difficult for us to continue to be confident of God's love – this is why we have brothers and sisters to strengthen us by reminding us of this irrevocable love. No one who believes (or claims to believe) what the Bible says would argue with the basic premise that God's thoughts are not our thoughts,[175] and no mature believer would judge the measure of God's love for someone by the difficult circumstances he is going through. When it comes to Israel, though, the majority of Christians sincerely believe they can reach conclusions about God's love based on things which are seen. For some reason they feel secure that His thoughts and theirs correspond exactly on this point. They base their judgments on the grounds of visible history and are absolutely convinced that this is how God thinks and feels concerning Israel. But indeed, His thoughts **are not** our thoughts, and if we truly love God we should seek to know His thoughts, His heart.

We will never be able to understand God by looking at just the things which are seen. A person who loves you differs from others in that often despite the outward conditions of your life, he sees all the way to your heart; your feelings and motives are transparent to him. Should not one who loves God strive for such an understanding? Do you remember Paul saying, *'For what man knows the things of a man except the spirit of the man which is in him? Even so no one knows the things of God except the Spirit of God.'*[176] Don't you have a burning desire to know His heart? He

---

[173] Rom. 8:38-39
[174] Heb. 11:1
[175] Is. 55:8
[176] 1 Cor. 2:11

reveals Himself not through the exterior circumstances of earthly history, but in the inner room, in His private chamber, in personal fellowship alone with the person praying. Those who love the Lord, who have experienced this fellowship and who meet with Him regularly in this inner room know how strikingly the things He reveals from heart to heart differ from human deductions based on visible events. We have received the Spirit of God, so let's trust Him to reveal His thoughts to us as we study His Word. Yes, the **visible** history of Israel throughout the past two thousand years is such that one must take great pains to not waver and to continue to believe in His love for His people; as in the story of Joseph, however, the truth is known only by the one who is able to see what is invisible.

Invisible tears

Unfortunately, as far as Israel goes, the overwhelming majority of people, including a huge majority of believers, prefer to be limited by this very same visible reality. It is especially tragic that not only the brothers but Benjamin himself does not see these invisible tears. Due to the terrible circumstances of our earthly history, not only does it appear to our enemies that the Lord has ceased loving Israel, but to us as well. It seems that He has abandoned His people, set them up if you will, and that He has given us over to abuse and pillaging. Many Jewish people perceive the suffering of our people in exactly this way. We can take as one example the words of Uri Tzvi Greenberg, the Israeli poet who survived the Holocaust and "called God to account." "Go to the other peoples," he writes, "to the *goyim,* leave us. You are not ours – You are theirs! They have been claiming for all these years that the Jewish people have no God and yes, after the Holocaust it became clear that they are right!" More than anything else on earth, this accusing voice longs to be wrong. So overflowing with pain, bitterness and resentment, how this voice longs to be refuted, to receive tangible proof of its error! Until the time comes that is set by God, however, the only thing that remains evident in the history of Israel is the cup in the sack. His passionate and unshakeable love for His people is hidden from human eyes and revealed only to those who meet with Him in Spirit in that inner room. Could Benjamin see the love in that cup placed in his sack? Even though in contrast to Benjamin, we the Jewish people do know Who the Author of our history is, we are often perplexed, not understanding how the history of our interminable sufferings and countless accusations could be the history of God's love for us –

A Palestinian terrorist blows up a school bus, and three children from the same family are left, all three of them, legless handicapped invalids – is this God's love? Another "holy martyr", having infiltrated a settlement, murders a mother and five of her eight children; of a happy family, looking out of a recent photograph with ten happy smiles, only a father frantic from grief and three wounded children remain – is this for what they were chosen? Israeli parents, taking their children abroad for a few days in order to give them a chance to rest from the terror of our daily reality on a paradisiacal Kenyan beach, return the next day with only one child, because two sons perished in the terrorist attack on the Kenyan hotel *Paradise* – and again, is this the Father's love? An elderly lady who had lost all of her family in the Holocaust brings her daughter and grandson to Israel – "so that nothing like that would ever happen to them" – and they both die in the explosion of a Jerusalem bus, leaving her barely alive in her grief, asking herself again and again if this was for what they were chosen. The space shuttle on which the first Israeli astronaut travels into space, for two weeks the only pride and joy of our people who in their suffering have long forgotten what joy is, explodes fifteen minutes before the end of the flight right over an American city called Palestine, to the delight and exultation of the entire Arab world, who see this as the sure hand of Allah – where, oh where? Where are the blessings God promised us? *My God, My God, why have You forsaken Me? Why are You so far from helping Me, and from the words of My groaning?*[177]

These frightening questions could go on forever, and despite all our human and completely natural hopes, unremitting groans

---

[177] Ps. 22:1

echo throughout Israel. Not long ago I heard a song in Hebrew, the first words of which were the famous *Shema Israel,*[178] except this time the words were addressed to the Lord: *Shema Israel, Adonai,* that is Lord, hear Israel – hear our cry, hear our moans, hear our prayer! These cries and prayers, this question full of unearthly torment again and again resounds in the heavenlies: where is Your love, Lord? Where are the *yearning of Your heart and Your mercies*[179] that You promised to your chosen and beloved people? Alas, too often God's love for Israel is **unseen** due to our innumerable tragedies. This is why it is so important to understand and remember the primary lesson of this chapter: **our visible history**, all the blood, the tears, the sorrows and suffering **is the outworking of His plan, not His feelings**; the separate fragments of our history do not say anything about His love for us. Only at the very end, when His plan is finally unfolded and complete, like Job chapter forty-two or Genesis chapter forty-five, only then will He **not be able to *restrain* Himself** and His love for us will become evident to all. In essence, this is true of all visible history, not just ours; however, in the case of Israel, beloved and chosen for sacrifice, this discrepancy between what He is doing and what He is feeling is truly great. It is just as in the case of Abraham, leading his beloved son to the sacrifice, or in the case of Joseph accusing his beloved brother of stealing.

Therefore, those who judge Israel based on what they see are unable to discern the love that makes the One leading us to the sacrifice weep in His *chamber,* out of sight. Similar to the brothers in the story of Joseph, they do not see reality, *they do not know the thoughts of the LORD, nor do they understand His counsel.*[180] Only the one who is able to see the unseen, the one to whom His tears for Israel are revealed in the inner room, the one who knows what torture it is for Him to withhold His compassion and mercy from His people – only this person can see Him as He really is. It is not as important to remember that it is the God of Israel allowing Israel to suffer, since this is quite plain to all.

---

178 "Hear, O Israel"; See Deuteronomy 6:4-9
179 Is. 63:15
180 Mic. 4:12

Everyone can see that the *yearning of [His] heart* and His *mercies* are often *restrained,*[181] and that Israel often seems to have been left by their God. It is more important to understand how much pain this causes Him. *'I have forsaken My house, I have left My heritage; I have given the dearly beloved of My soul into the hand of her enemies.'*[182] The God of Israel has not left and despised, has not forgotten or ceased loving His firstborn as many claim, pointing often gloatingly to the suffering Israel. He loves Israel today with that same undying, eternal love. *'Can a woman forget her nursing child, and not have compassion on the son of her womb? Surely they may forget, yet I will not forget you.'*[183] But, similar to Joseph, throughout the course of our earthly history He has withheld from showing His love. Therefore, through the mirror-like image revealed by this chapter He wants to show you and me what the rest cannot see: He wants to show us His tears. He wants us to see how the God of Israel is weeping in the inner room out of love for His people and how, *restraining* **Himself** (nearly wiping the tears from His face), **He withholds His love,** as Joseph withheld his love for Benjamin. Yes, for the time being He withholds His love… for the sake of His plan.

❃ ❃ ❃

Unfulfilled expectations

So what is this plan that is so painful for us? What plan could be so important that its reflection and expression became such a tragic **visible history** for us? In the Gospel of Luke there is a verse which for us, the Messianic Jewish believers in Yeshua, is doubtless one of the most poignant verses there is: *then passing through the midst of them, He went His way.*[184] With God's help, we will answer the crucial question of how Yeshua, who *was not sent except to the lost sheep of the house of Israel,*[185] could then pass

---

[181] Is. 63:15
[182] Jer. 12:7
[183] Is. 49:15
[184] Luke 4:30
[185] Mat. 15:24

through the midst of them, and go *His way.* Was this the result of our sin, our falling away and our ruining of God's plan, or was this His original design for Israel and the nations?

The main accusation of the Christian world against Israel, the accusation lying at the foundation of all other reproaches and rebukes, is that the Jewish people did not recognize their Messiah and rejected and crucified Him. The majority of Christians through the ages have been taught that Jesus of Nazareth fulfilled the Messianic prophecies of the *Tenach,* and that the fact that the Jewish people did not recognize Him can be understood only as a result of their spiritual blindness. There has been a growing recognition in recent years, however, that this commonly held view was heavily influenced by early anti-Semitic Christian theologians. While what I say now might seem heretical to some of my brethren in the faith, it is not only I who believe that it is the truth in the sight of God, but by the Spirit of God today it is also becoming clearer to an increasingly greater number of Christian theologians and scholars.

Reading the Gospels with believing eyes and a believing heart, seeing Yeshua performing miracles, healing the sick and proclaiming the Kingdom of God, one can really wonder how it could be possible not to recognize God's Messenger, filled with such authority and grace. If we shift perspectives, however, and are able to look at Yeshua not from here and now, through the gospel text and our God-revealed faith but through the eyes of His contemporaries and fellow-countrymen, if we can see Him against the backdrop of Israel at that time and the Messianic expectations of the day and compare His ministry and message with these expectations – we begin to understand that it was by no means as overwhelmingly easy to recognize Him as it seems to us today.

Remember the very last question the disciples asked Yeshua here on the earth? This one question is enough to understand how great the difference was between the redemption Israel was looking for and that which Yeshua brought. Open the Book of Acts and in the very beginning, in the scene preceding His ascension, you will read: *'Lord, will You at this time restore the kingdom to Israel?'*[186] Please note that they are asking this not only after three years of uninterrupted fellowship with Him, but **after** His death on the cross and resurrection, after the forty days He had appeared to them, teaching and explaining the mysteries of God's plan to them. Theirs was a typical question; the Messiah that Israel was waiting for couldn't help but bring redemption and salvation to the people of Israel. If after all His explanations and messages, the disciples He had chosen and instructed continued to expect this from Him, then what does this say about all the other multitudes of Israelites who, listening to His messages and seeing His miracles, were absolutely convinced that sooner or later He would be sure to begin saving and restoring Israel?

Faith in a kingly Messiah who would restore the throne of David and hence the *kingdom to Israel,* was an inseparable component of faith in God, and was based on a Biblical promise. *'I will set up your seed after you, who will come from your body, and I will establish his kingdom. He shall build a house for My name, and I will establish the throne of his kingdom forever. I will be his Father, and he shall be My son.'*[187] In this context, **the Messiah-King,** *Mashiach ben-David*, was understood to be the one who would come primarily to fulfill this purpose. No devout, believing person in Israel could imagine that God would send His salvation by a savior that would not save His people. Yeshua, as we all know, wasn't sent to restore the kingdom of Israel, and therefore didn't come in accordance with normal Jewish Messianic expectations. He ascended the altar, not the throne of David. He wasn't sent to restore the people of Israel as was expected of the Messiah, and in this sense all the Messianic promises that Israel associated with the coming of the Messiah in fact remained unfulfilled during the time of His first coming. The fulfillment of these Biblical promises lies secure in the future, as they are part of God's unalterable Word. It is vital, however, to realize that because they remained unfulfilled during Yeshua's first coming, the only people in Israel who could recognize Him as the Messiah were the ones to whom the Lord Himself desired to

---

[186] Acts 1:6
[187] 2 Sam. 7:12-14

reveal it by His Spirit. *'Blessed are you, Simon Bar-Jonah, for flesh and blood has not revealed this to you, but My Father who is in heaven.'* [188] When speaking to Peter, Yeshua knew very well the truth that today we are only beginning to realize: that by human means, by *flesh and blood,* Israel had no chance of discovering of His Messianic identity.

We have come to a tremendously significant juncture. Do you remember that we earlier spoke of a pier-glass and of many mirror-like reflections, each of which, though fully adequate in itself, at the same time inevitably reflects only a small part of the entire object? The images contained in this book were revealed to me as only a selection of many possible reflections and refractions of His mystery concerning Israel and salvation, but I am convinced that it is extremely important to the Lord that this particular revelation be seen and grasped by believers today. This reflected fragment that I am proclaiming, one of the aspects of God's plan, not only required for Israel as a people to be unable to recognize Yeshua as the Messiah, but also for them to be **not supposed to recognize Him.** Before getting all indignant and disagreeing, consider how two different people looking into one and the selfsame mirror can be viewing it at completely different angles and accordingly, they will see the same object reflected completely differently, from totally differing perspectives. This is what is happening as you begin to comprehend this revelation: you are unexpectedly seeing our subject from a new angle and in a different light, even though you never imagined you could find anything unexpected in it. It is not my intention to prove anything to anyone; I place my trust in the Word of God, through which His mysteries are revealed, and in the Spirit of God, who will Himself confirm to your hearts what is of Him, even when it is difficult to accept due to the limitations of human logic.

---

[188] Mat. 16:17

Yeshua's hidden identity

Curiously enough, Yeshua did not refer to Himself as the "Messiah" during His earthly ministry, continually calling himself *the Son of Man*. This very special spiritual title taken from the prophet Daniel (*'I was watching in the might visions, and behold, One like the Son of Man, coming with the clouds of heaven!'*[189]) hardly coincided with Messianic ideas or expectations of the time. Moreover, Yeshua directly forbade others to speak of Him as the Messiah. *He said to them, 'But who do you say that I am?' Peter answered and said, 'The Christ* [Messiah] *of God.' And He strictly warned and commanded them to tell this to no one.*[190] The only time in the entire New Testament that He reveals his Messianic identity is in the scene with the Samaritan woman in John chapter four. Just consider it! The only time when He speaks of it, it is not to a Jewish person but to a Samaritan woman, and even then only at the moment when *His disciples had gone away into the city to buy food,*[191] that is, when there was not a single Jewish person in sight!

A similar ban accompanies all His healings of Israelites: the cleansing of the leper, the raising of Jairus' daughter from the dead, the healing of the blind... These and many other stories are almost unavoidably accompanied by a concluding commentary: *and He **strictly** warned him... and said to him, 'See that you say nothing to anyone;'*[192] *but He commanded them **strictly** that no one should know it;*[193] *and Jesus **sternly** warned them, saying, 'See that no one knows it.'*[194] He didn't just recommend that they not say anything – He forbade them to talk about it, and almost always **strictly.** Isn't it curious that this word strictly, when used in the Gospels, is only found in this context? The only thing that Yeshua did **sternly** was to forbid people to discuss His Messianic

---

[189] Dan. 7:13
[190] Luke 9:20-21
[191] John 4:8
[192] Mark 1:43-44
[193] Mark 5:43
[194] Mat. 9:30

identity and miracles and to me, ignoring this fact shows great disrespect to the Word of God. To this day neither preachers nor scholars have given us an intelligible explanation about this peculiarity of Yeshua's ministry. Let's look at an additional curious detail that must be taken into account: in the same way Yeshua reveals His closely guarded identity to the Samaritan woman, the healing of the demon-possessed man from the Gentile country of the Gadarenes also contrasts greatly all these stories quoted above with their prohibitions of advertising the healings. In answer to his request to follow Him, Yeshua tells the healed man, *'Go home to your friends, and tell them what great things the Lord has done for you, and how He has had compassion on you.'*[195]

We are now faced with the necessity of explaining a rather curious fact: in all four Gospels, not once does Yeshua reveal Himself as Messiah to His fellow-countrymen (the Father's revelation and the confession of Peter is a different case, and we will speak of this further on). In all four Gospels, the Jewish people He heals are not allowed to tell about the miracles done for them. Why? Is it not logical to conclude that He did not intend to reveal the fact of His Messianic identity to His people? Otherwise, why would He Himself not speak about this directly, instead forbidding people to tell others? If we decide that the will of God for Israel was to accept and recognize Yeshua as Messiah, then we must admit that Yeshua was doing all He could in order to lead Israel into error and hide this secret from them. You must agree that such a conclusion is hardly acceptable, and consequently we are left with only one possibility: that the mystery of God's plan for Israel was such that Israel was not supposed to have (yes, not supposed to have!) recognized Yeshua as the Messiah. Let me repeat: **Israel was looking for a King who would ascend the throne. The Messiah turned out to be a sacrificial Lamb who ascended the altar.** *Then I said, 'Behold, I come; in the scroll of the book it is written of me. I delight to do Your will, O my God.'*[196] The fact that Yeshua came to give Himself as an offering surpassed all human expectations and understanding, and for this reason not *flesh and*

---

[195] Mark 5:19
[196] Ps. 40:7-8

blood but only the *Father who is in heaven*[197] could reveal this to a heart by His Spirit.

Sprinkled with blood

The chapters to which the Lord is now directing me from the first section of the Book of *Vayikra*,[198] contain the directions for various sacrificial offerings and are not necessarily the most well-loved, well-read, or often-quoted in the Bible. I even suspect that many of my readers have not perused them for quite some time, and yet He is now leading me to speak about the bloody labor of the priest whose job it was to perform the sacrifices. Those who come to God in search of purely spiritual sensations will be patently discouraged by these pages: reading them is akin to a stroll through a butcher's shop – here they speak of the fat, the "fat tail", the kidneys, the "fatty lobe", the liver and especially… the blood. A lot of blood. These are very bloody pages because, in accordance with God's injunctions, the tasks and ministry of the priest dealt daily in blood.

> *The anointed priest shall bring some of the bull's blood to the tabernacle of meeting. Then the priest shall dip his finger in the blood and sprinkle it seven times before the LORD, in front of the veil. And he shall put some of the blood on the horns of the altar which is before the LORD, which is in the tabernacle of meeting; and he shall pour the remaining blood at the base of the altar of burnt offering, which is at the door of the tabernacle of meeting… And he shall do with the bull as he did with the bull as a sin offering; thus he shall do with it. So the priest shall make atonement for them, and it shall be forgiven them.*[199]

The above passage is only one of many sacrifices, one of many continuously repeated episodes. During the first seven chapters

---

[197] Mat. 16:17
[198] The Hebrew name for the Book of Leviticus
[199] Lev. 4:16-20

of the Book of Leviticus we see the priest at the altar over and over again; we watch as he slays the sacrifice and sprinkles the altar with blood. Once in some history book I read how the priest, having finished with the sacrifice, would turn to the people waiting for him (at least this was how it was done in past centuries, during the Second Temple Period) and lifting his hands, would bless those present. From that time on, I have always pictured those bloody hands facing the people in blessing – the hands of the one who had just slain the innocent sacrifice in obedience to God.

Aware of everything that has taken place since that time, and coming to understand the progressive unfolding of God's plan of redemption, it is impossible to read these lines without trembling inwardly. So many detailed directions are given by God even before the first priest is anointed for ministry that essentially, they forestall the beginning of the priestly ministry that only begins in the eighth chapter of Leviticus. The ministry of the priests began in the desert tabernacle. Hundreds of years later after the Temple was built, this ministry was transferred to the Temple and became an integral part of it. After that time the only true and right sacrifice was considered to be one made at the Temple, while everything that came before was seen as simply a type of the temple sacrifices. In this way the Temple as a place of sacrifice became the next step in the unfolding of God's plan. (It is for this reason that sacrificial offerings totally ceased following the destruction of the Second Temple. None of the Jewish sages could even imagine returning to God's earlier ways and to what existed in the pre-Temple era.) At last, the final stage arrived with the coming of the *One greater than the temple*.[200] Many years after all these directions were originally given, we see the once-for-all, final Sacrifice of the Son of God, of which all the earlier ones were a *copy and shadow*.[201] In this sacrifice, the Heavenly Father Himself took up the role of the priest in order to slay the Son who had taken the place of the sacrificial offering. In the sacrifices in the Book of Leviticus, there are two participants – the priest and the sacrifice itself; Golgotha

---

[200] Mat. 12:6
[201] Heb. 8:5

repeats this same scene, only this time it is not just an anonymous priest sacrificing an innocent animal for some unknown person's sin, but rather God Himself offering up His Son for the sins of each of us. For two thousand years now, the Father has continued to bless the world with those bloodied outstretched hands with which He offered up His Son. He blesses us by showing this blood to the very humans for the sake of whose salvation the offering was slain. *It is finished!*[202]

In this particular Biblical context and in such a sense, the famous Gospel scene of Yeshua's sentencing is filled with special meaning. *Pilate... took water and washed his hands before the multitude, saying, 'I am innocent of the blood of this just Person. You see to it.' And all the people answered and said, 'His blood be on us and on our children.'*[203] Washing his hands and showing them to the witnesses standing there, Pilate did the exact opposite of what a priest would do when performing a sacrifice, in this way unwittingly and graphically demonstrating that he was not the priest officiating at God's sacrifice. Not that he was absolved of responsibility on the human level, exactly the thing he was trying to deny, but in the sense that he truly did not have a part in the deeper spiritual significance of the proceedings; on the spiritual level he was not a player in this sacrifice. Instead, the priestly role is filled by the Heavenly Father Himself, offering His Son on the altar. Israel, however, *('His blood be on us and on our children')* was allotted a very difficult and special role. We were chosen to play the part of the altar, which is inevitably sprinkled with the blood of the sacrifice. *In the place where they kill the burnt offering they shall kill the trespass offering. **And its blood he shall sprinkle all around on the altar.***[204] The blood of the lamb has forever remained on us.

This is the unfathomable Sacrifice that was the deepest, most intimate part in God's plan, so extraordinary that before

---

[202] John 19:30
[203] Mat. 27:24-25
[204] Lev. 7:2

Yeshua's coming it was not revealed to anyone and completely concealed from Israel. It was not that Israel didn't wish to see it, but God Himself chose not to reveal it until the *fullness of the time had come.*[205] The Lord Himself decided not to reveal to Israel that the coming Messiah would become the sacrificial Lamb and this is why Israel, waiting for their Messiah, was in no way expecting someone who would come and lay His life down on the altar. Israel was waiting for a Messiah, but for a King who would ascend the throne of David, not a Lamb that would ascend to a bloody pedestal to be slain.

Enemies... for your sake

It is very important that we catch hold of this concept. Many times in their history, the people of Israel were stiff-necked and committed spiritual adultery. Yes, we worshipped idols and turned away from the living God, but not once was this God's plan for us, for Israel. It was always our sinful choice for which His punishment followed. According to Paul, however, the whole plan involving Yeshua was God's plan for Israel, the very plan through which *the depth of the riches both of the wisdom and knowledge of God*[206] would be revealed, and this should be enough to see that our two thousand years of suffering could not be merely punishment. The Lord could not punish us for what He Himself had purposed for us! According to what has been revealed to me in our dim looking glass, my people not only **could not** recognize Him but moreover, were **not supposed to** recognize Him – and this is one of the things we were chosen for!

Chosen to not recognize? Yes, chosen to reflect the Light that came into the world, so that it could go out from us and light up the darkest corners of the globe. Recall the distinctive way Paul formulates this thought: *concerning the gospel they are enemies for your sake.*[207] *Enemies* – this is the people of Israel; *for your sake* –

[205] Gal. 4:4
[206] Rom. 11:33
[207] Rom. 11:28

e nations, the Gentiles; *the gospel* – this is the
ting off Israel, has gone into all the world. We
ustration to clarify this concept. If someone is
ight down from above and once it reaches the
it it to stay at one point but to be scattered
...ace, he must find some point from which the beam
can be refracted. This point itself, however, will remain without
light. This is the task for which we were chosen: *concerning the
gospel... enemies for your sake.* The Lord has made us "enemies",
unable to receive but instead reflecting that Light so that other
peoples might benefit from it. This inanimate illustration,
however, does not convey the heavy burden and incredible
sorrow that accompanies such a plan. At some point those who
are swept up in this light are sure to turn against the point left
without light, though they received the light thanks to it. This is
the story of our history. The One who sent the Light originally
designed us for this purpose and has made us enemies Himself
for their sake, since the Light could simply not reach other
regions if we had no ability to reflect. Whether forgetting this or
consciously not desiring to know it, Christians quickly and
furiously began to accuse Israel of rejecting and not desiring to
receive the Light that the Christians had received. In this sense,
Yeshua's coming put Israel in a situation analogous to the one
into which Benjamin ended up at the hands of Joseph – accused
of something that is primarily the responsibility of the plan's
Author. God's original intent was that Israel should but reflect
the Light and not recognize it save for a remnant, to whom as
Paul writes, *it pleased God... to reveal His Son*[208] – and in complete
harmony with this plan, Yeshua came in such a way that Israel
would not be able to recognize Him as the Messiah.

For the sake of the plan

Now we can finally answer the question of why Yeshua forbade
people to tell others about His Messianic identity. Revealing that
Yeshua was the Messiah to the Israelites would be similar to

---

[208] Gal. 1:15-16

Joseph's steward, having searched the brothers and found the cup in Benjamin's sack, at that point telling them how and why the cup got there. Joseph's entire plan would have been ruined and would simply not have worked. The test created by Joseph could yield the desired effect only because neither Benjamin nor his brothers knew the truth at that moment. Similarly, the plan of salvation fashioned by the Lord was possible only because Israel did not know this truth, necessitating that Yeshua forbid the advertising of His secret Messianic identity. In the story of Benjamin this lack of knowledge continued for a few hours, but in the history of Israel it has lasted for two thousand years, inscribed on the bloodiest and most frightening pages in the history of Israel. Just as in these several hours Benjamin was made out to be the "thief", so in our bloody story we carry the widely-accepted horrifying title of "Christ-killers". For two thousand years we have borne this accusation: the cup is extracted from the bag, Benjamin-Israel remains silent in the face of the condemning looks of his brothers, and only his bleeding heart silently cries to the Lord, *'My God, My God, why have You forsaken Me?'*[209]

"Wait a minute!" – somebody might say. "Could the Lord really choose Israel for such a task, His beloved people whom He calls His son? Could it possibly be that after all this you are still trying to say that He continues to love the people of Israel?" Indeed, we would not have been able to fully comprehend Israel's history, their apparently being caught "red-handed" as it were, if the Lord had not revealed His plans to us beforehand in the story of Joseph. Those who do not know the heart of the Lord might consider Him to have abandoned and "framed" His people, but we who have seen His tears for Israel **in the inner room,** will never again doubt His love. Did Joseph not love Benjamin? I believe that the Lord directed me to write this chapter, and indeed this whole book, to show that **only the love of God is capable of placing the one it loves on the altar.** This entire book is about the love of God for Israel and the mysteries of His plan. It might not be easy for us, the children of Israel, to hear it, but

---

[209] Ps. 22:1

nothing proves the love of God for His people more than His willingness, having **restrained** **Himself,** to lay Israel on the altar. In Jewish literature, in the *Midrash,* we often come across a scene in which Satan tries to convince Abraham not to sacrifice Isaac. It is very similar to the New Testament passage where, frightened about the future sufferings of Yeshua, Simon Peter *took Him aside and began to rebuke Him, saying, 'Far be it from You, Lord; this shall not happen to You!'* The Lord says to Peter, *'Get behind Me, Satan! You are an offense to Me, for you are not mindful of the things of God, but the things of men.'*[210] Naturally speaking, it is very difficult to write about such an election and calling for my people, but we know full well who it is that causes us think about *the things of the flesh.* On the other hand, if we think about *the things of the Spirit,*[211] we can accept the truth that the most magnificent and awe-inspiring plans of God are always connected with sacrifice. And for such a sacrifice, the Lord always gives His best and most precious possession.

✖ ✖ ✖

Separated from the peoples

Just a few more words about the brothers must be said before we conclude this chapter. We have already spoken about the drastic contrast in the relationship between Benjamin and his brothers that can be observed in the scene with the cup: the one who in the eyes of his brothers was separated from them all these years by his innocence, righteousness and consequent closeness to God is now suddenly separated from them by guilt and sin. All this time they have had to deal with the annoying fact of his righteousness (when compared with them), but now, finally, the tables are turned and they are the righteous ones, he the sinner. Just as Joseph does, you and I know that in reality he is guilty of nothing, but since his purity all these years had released in them far from the purest of feelings, this distinctive division now created by the fabricated crime is greeted with enthusiasm. The

---

[210] Mat. 16:22-23
[211] Rom. 8:5

greater the fury with which they betray their resentment and displeasure, however, the more they understand in the depth of their hearts that something is not right about this situation.

For two thousand years this motif has sounded through the history of Israel. Starting from the time of Abraham, Israel has been the people of God – a nation the Lord separated from other nations, took for Himself and called His own. *'And you shall be holy to Me, for I the LORD am holy, and have separated you from the peoples, that you should be Mine.'*[212] In Hebrew the word קדוש (holy) also means "separated", and therefore the words את מקודשת לי repeated by the groom to the bride in the Jewish wedding ceremony, or *hupa,* simultaneously mean "you are separated to me" and "you are holy to me." They impart the very essence of this love that chooses and separates someone for itself. It is logical that the pagan peoples who did not believe in a monotheistic God could not seriously appreciate or accept God's election of Israel, but at the same time Israel's dissimilarity from other peoples was an obvious fact which, one way or another, it was necessary to acknowledge: *a people dwelling alone, not reckoning itself among the nations.*[213] Yes, the Gentile nations have always sensed that Israel was a special people, different, separated from all other nations. Perhaps this is the reason that the very Gentiles who through the death and resurrection of Yeshua had received access to the God of Israel rushed to denounce our people as forever guilty, cursed and outcast in the eyes of God (our own God!), hurrying to again turn us into a nation separated from all others, except this time separated by our crime.

Discovering the truth

Joseph needed the set-up with Benjamin in order for the brothers to repent, be transformed and cleansed, and so that the dialogue with God in their hearts could be completed and bring forth its

---

[212] Lev. 20:26
[213] Num. 23:9

fruit. Why did the Lord need to set Israel up, and what is His plan for us? The Word of God gives us a full and direct answer to this question: *enemies for your sake.*[214] The Lord gives His beloved son Israel to be an enemy and prisoner *for your sake,* in order that the Gentile nations could come to know the one true God, in order for them to be saved and cleansed, so that the salvation by grace He had prepared for the world could be offered to them. The people who received salvation due to our role as enemies are being tested with Israel today. The testing of Benjamin's brothers was possible only because Joseph's love for Benjamin was hidden from them. Without exception, each brother had to be kept in the dark regarding the infinite love the powerful governor, whom they were all afraid of and depended on, held for their younger brother – and this is how their true attitude towards him could be ascertained. In the same way, the attitude of the nations toward Israel can be assessed and gauged because on the level of **visible** circumstances, absolutely nothing is coercing them to believe that God loves His people. (It goes without saying that those who know God loves Israel can find enough visible confirmations of this love; however, the innumerable tragic facts of our history are also at the service of those who claim that God has rejected the chosen people.) As always, God gives everyone a free choice, and in this case the liberty to choose one's attitude to Benjamin-Israel. Paradoxically, it is by this attitude that He will judge whether or not the nations' attitudes towards Him are genuine, and whether they are sincere in their worship of Him.

Do you remember the first conversation Joseph had with his brothers? The ten brothers stand before Joseph, bowing down to the ground before him, and he tells them no, I will not speak with you until you bring your younger brother. Moreover, specifically by your bringing him with you will I discover *whether there is any truth in you,* whether you have come to me in sincerity, and have sincerely repented before me. *In this manner you shall be tested: ...bring your brother... that your words may be tested to see **whether there is any truth in you.***[215] The nations

---

[214] Rom. 11:28
[215] Gen. 42:15-16

100

considering themselves to be "Christian", when standing before His throne, will be surprised to hear, "Bring Me your brother – and I will *see whether there is any truth in you;* if not, then it means that everything you have told Me, all your faith and your service is simply not truth!"

When commenting on the dramatic meeting between Benjamin and Joseph, preachers like to point out how Benjamin-Israel was finally able to recognize his brother. It is impossible not to agree; Israel, who has not known Yeshua, will be amazed to discover the loving brother in the One who always seemed so much the stranger and enemy. The meeting of Benjamin and Joseph is a truly poignant and beautiful image of that future meeting. But have you ever considered that it was not only Benjamin who did not recognize Joseph upon meeting him, but all the other brothers as well? The brothers here represent the nations surrounding Israel, the very peoples who in complete agreement with prophecy received the Light reflected from Israel and obtained the mercy, grace and salvation of God – and who for so long have despised the one thanks to whom they received this Light. If we follow the logic of the image, then not only Israel but all the Christian nations as well do not really recognize Yeshua. Imagine, millions of people considering themselves Christians who upon meeting Him won't even recognize Him, signifying that in reality they did not actually know the Jesus they had supposedly been serving. For this reason I am convinced that the story of the meeting between Joseph and his brothers needs to be read by the Church not only with a triumphant gaze fixed on Israel ("Ah," they say, "the time will come when you will finally recognize Him!"), but with searching thoughts and prayers for themselves, "Will we recognize Him?" "Do we really know Him?" "Do we know His heart?" Believers are obliged to ask themselves these questions because even today their hearts are being tested concerning the one who is so dear to His heart.

The scapegoat

We may note that the Biblical text does not characterize Benjamin even with a single word. We really don't know whether he is righteous or sinful, whether he is faithful to God or has transgressed in some ways, but judging by this lack of information it must not be so critical to our story. What is important, however, is to remember that the scheme with the cup placed in Benjamin's sack is in no way connected with his hypothetical sins. I am sure that he did have sins, *for there is no one who does not sin.*[216] Joseph's plot was not planned as punishment for these sins, however. Rather, it was only born out of his love for Benjamin and from his desire to see the hearts of the brothers renewed and transformed.

Benjamin, to his horror and bewilderment, is in some sense the "scapegoat" of the story, on top of which the only reason for his being chosen for such a dubious honor is that among all the brothers he is especially dear. He is Joseph's beloved brother and therefore used as the bait to test his brothers. Although it goes without saying that Benjamin's heart does change through this test, it is not his heart that is the primary object being tested with this story. It is not for his sake that everything is happening, yet the most difficult and painful role must be played by him.

Israel is also by no means the only one being tested with this two-thousand-year-old story, yet the people of Israel are the ones who carry the full burden of the humiliation of being the "bait". Whatever the situation may be, and however much we try to be strong or be *like all the other nations,*[217] this role or this *place,* as Job called it, of the one in whose sack the cup is placed, or whose sufferings are interpreted as God's punishment, or who is accused of the "murder of the Lord" – is a dreadful place. The *Place of a Skull.*[218]

---

[216] 1 Kings 8:46
[217] 1 Sam. 8:5
[218] John 19:17

He is waiting

It is my belief that as in the story of Joseph, the revelation of Yeshua to Israel will become possible only after the nations are tested specifically with what is the nearest and dearest to His heart. When we finally witness the willingness of Gentiles to lay down their life for Israel, then the end is truly near. Only when Christians understand that He is not only waiting for them but for their brother as well (because he is His brother!), when they are ready to return for their brother and are willing to again walk out the entire path, when they are ready to entreat the Father and become a guarantee for Israel as the brothers were for Benjamin, when they are finally ready to lay down their life for this brother – then He will no longer be able to restrain Himself. Then He will reveal Himself to his brothers, falling on the neck of "Benjamin" and weeping. Then the time will come it speaks of when, *'I will pour on the house of David and on the inhabitants of Jerusalem the Spirit of grace and supplication; then they will look on Me whom they pierced. Yes, they will mourn for Him as one mourns for his only son, and grieve for Him as one grieves for a firstborn.'*[219]

Yes, the plan of the Lord with Israel, just as the plan of Joseph with Benjamin, is such that it is difficult for the brothers to resist the temptation to accuse the innocent. It was not Joseph's desire that Benjamin stand accused, although the cup was found in his sack. It is not God's desire, either, that Israel stand accused, although it was in the land of Israel that the One died who was destined to suffer for the sins of the world and thus fulfill the plan of salvation. Rather, our Father desires for believers to repent and to open their hearts to both God's love for His people and His conviction. *'God has found out the iniquity of your servants.'*[220] This is what will open the door for us all to enter into God's glory.

This day, a *day which is known to the LORD,*[221] will surely come. The Lord is looking forward to this day no less than you or I,

---

[219] Zech. 12:10
[220] Gen. 44:16
[221] Zech. 14:7

waiting just as Joseph waited for the repentance of the brothers. He is waiting for the desire of His heart: the day when He can reveal Himself to His beloved people and hold them close to His heart. In that day the Lord Himself *will wipe away every tear*[222] from the eyes of Israel. In that day, He promises us that *you will ask Me nothing.*[223] Meanwhile, since His plan is not yet finished, His love is currently revealed only in the "inner room". Now is the time that we can ask and that He will answer. Everything I have written in this book, the Lord has spoken to me as His answer to many years of questioning the suffering of Israel. It is my prayer and hope that I will not be the only one for whom this book becomes the answer sought from the Lord.

---

[222] Rev. 21:4
[223] John 16:23

CHAPTER THREE

And He said, "Where have you laid him?"
They said to Him, "Lord, come and see."
Jesus wept. Then the Jews said, "See how
He loved him!" (John 11:34-36)

Now as He drew near, He saw the city
and wept over it. (Luke 19:41)

Originally, I had wavered between calling the introductory pages of this book on Isaac's sacrifice chapter one or the foreword, until the Lord inscribed across my mind's eye the word **Prologue.** Analogous to how the leaves, branches and trunk of a future tree are captured in the seed from which it grows, each thought or image revealed by the Holy Spirit in the chapters that follow is already contained within this story that was enacted before the beginning of time and still echoes from beyond its limits. In this way, the prologue is the binding that holds the entire book together. It is possible that literary specialists will not agree with me; perhaps in the strict sense of the term, a prologue should simply describe the events preceding the main action of a book, to some degree providing the reason behind it. This prologue, on the other hand, though its action does indeed precede that of the following chapters, expresses everything I have been given to say here in a concentrated form. Akin to the sound of the *shofar*[224] on the eve

---

[224] Traditional trumpet made from a ram's horn

of *Rosh Hashanah* when the *Akedah* is read in synagogues around the world, or to the piercing, melancholy cry of a lone seagull lost over a boundless autumn sea, or perhaps to the plaintive wails of a sleeping child that break the heart with their helpless and bitter insecurity – echoing off the halls of eternity, the unspeakably mournful melody emanating from Mount Moriah seizes the soul with its unbearable beauty. In each of this book's chapters the separate notes of the original refrain are sounded out, and our ears take each of them in individually. Help me, dear Lord, to impart this music! Help me to preserve and not detract from the inner oneness of such seemingly different themes, which in accordance with Your design miraculously merge into a united whole!

The word the Lord has given me concerning Israel can be seen clearly only as a composite image. Were any of the voices to be omitted, the overall melody would be indiscernible. When taken alone, none of these chapters express enough of the fullness I want to share, just as in only a single leaf of a looking-glass one cannot see an object from all sides. Each leaf of a hinged mirror displays its own perspective, compounding and completing the reflection of the original object and correspondingly, each chapter included here executes its own motif. We are now beginning a new chapter and it is not without trepidation that we uncover yet another facet of our looking glass: what will we see in the mirror this time? Which of the echoes resonating from this amazing melody lingers on these next pages?

Above all that we ask or think

Do you remember some of the first words the God of Israel used to address the people He had just led out of Egypt? *In the third month after the children of Israel had gone out of the land of Egypt,* the Lord spoke to them saying, *'If you will indeed obey My voice and keep My covenant, then you shall be a special treasure to Me above all people; for all the earth is Mine. And you shall be to Me a kingdom of priests and a holy nation.'*[225] Just imagine: questioning, doubting, often simply complaining, for the third month in a row this exhausted band of people has been plodding through the desert on their seemingly endless journey. (What would they have said if they knew they still had forty years ahead of them?!) They had forsaken Egypt and followed the Lord, or Moses, rather, who was leading them in His steps. They probably felt that the time had come to reap the rewards of their obedience, but what did they get as their reward? What did the God who led them out of Egypt promise them?

One of the first verses that the Lord ever used to speak to me is the famous verse from Ephesians which says He is able to do *exceedingly abundantly above all that we ask or think.*[226] I am sure that these powerful words have spoken to your heart numerous times as well. Naturally, when reading this promise we like to believe that *exceedingly above* is referring to a greater amount of all we desire: abundant health, prosperity and success, not to mention an abundance of spiritual blessings, as well: our loved ones we have been praying for will come to the faith more quickly, greater numbers of people will repent, and so on. For a long time I also took the verse this way, and of course such things do take place and very often at that. Every believer has come to know their Heavenly Father in this capacity, pouring out on us the blessings we dreamed about and prayed for, only in exceeding greater abundance than we could imagine. I am convinced, though, that the original and central reference to God's *exceedingly above* refers to a difference in quality; at the outset the words *exceedingly above*[227] reveal that there is an irreconcilable disparity between what we understand as being good for us and what He wants to give us for our good.

The *exceedingly above* of the Lord is truly superior to what we can imagine. It belongs to a place we usually don't arrive at in our meditations because it is our nature to seek out the things that

---

[225] Ex. 19:1,5,6

[226] Eph. 3:20

[227] The Greek word, *huper,* translated here as *exceedingly above,* has also been translated in this verse as *more* (NIV), *far more… beyond* (NASB), and *far over and above, infinitely beyond* (AMP).

are good for our body and soul, whereas the Lord offers something *above* that: He gives us what is good for our spirit. Do you recall how Esau despised his birthright? He came home from hunting and was exceptionally famished, and really wanted some of the stew his brother had made. When Jacob offered to give him the soup in exchange for his birthright, Esau said, *'Look, I am about to die; so what is this birthright to me?'*[228] (It should be noted here that his life was in absolutely no danger at that moment – all his "dying" consisted of being very, very hungry and nothing worse than that was threatening him.) I'm hungry – so what do I need spiritual blessings for? Who can think of a birthright at a time like this? Give me a break! It is probable that the people the Lord led into the desert would have said something along these lines. We are hungry and tired, why bother us with Your holiness? Wandering through the desert, their thoughts could go no higher than eating and drinking. *Exceedingly above* for them meant more food, and through the provision of quail a few days before, God quite convincingly proved the ease with which He is able to give *exceedingly above* what human understanding allows people to expect from Him. His plan didn't stop there, however. This was not all He had prepared for His people; His purpose in leading them out of Egypt was something much greater indeed. This is why He spoke such marvelous words to the hungry, haggard wanderers who only dreamed of filling their stomachs and getting some rest, and were far from contemplating the benefits of holiness. He proposed something way beyond rest and food: He offered the homeless the opportunity to become His *special treasure;* He promised to make the poor a *kingdom of priests* and to form the disgruntled into a *holy nation.* This was *exceedingly abundantly above* all that they could *ask or think,* and how difficult it was for them to accept this *exceedingly above* that the Lord had for them!

---

[228] Gen. 25:32

Here I am

Let's take another look at our Prologue, at the lines of the *Akedah*. At the opening of *Bereshit* chapter twenty-two where Abraham's test begins, the Lord calls to him, '*Abraham!*' – to which Abraham readily replies הנני or '*Here I am.*'

Wisely and with the remotest of irony, the *Midrash's* commentary expands his answer: הנני לכהונה הנני למלכות - "Here I am for the priesthood; here I am for the kingdom."[229]

What does this imply? Simply that after all of God's promises to him, Abraham was not able at that moment to imagine what the Lord was going to require of him. He responds immediately to the call, but responds to "the priesthood", to "the kingdom", convinced in his heart that this was what he was being called to. Abraham stayed faithful to his call, however, even when he found out to what the Lord had really called him. He did not doubt or hesitate even when he discovered how terrible a price he would have to pay for his faithfulness. This is why Abraham became the father of a nation and many nations; this is why he is Avraam Avinu – אברעם אבינו – "Abraham our father".

At times, the same thing happens in each of our lives. The Lord calls us and in all readiness we respond to His call, confident of our election and the high calling accorded by this election. "Here I am for the priesthood; here I am for the kingdom." Similar to the disciples in Matthew chapter twenty, *kneeling down and asking something,* we are doling out portions of the honor, figuring out our share in God's kingdom – and suddenly, amidst the flurry of these preparations, we are shaken by His quiet voice. '*You do not know what you ask. Are you able to drink the cup that I am about to drink, and be baptized with the baptism that I am baptized with?*'[230] This is to what He has called us: to drink the cup that He drinks, the same cup He asked that *if it is possible, let this cup pass from*

---

[229] *Midrash Raba Bereshit,* parashah 55
[230] Mat. 20:22

Me,[231] and it is this calling that sadly few agree to. *Many are called, but few chosen.*[232] The Lord has called many by name, and many in readiness answer, *'Here I am ,'* but few are the Abrahams who remain faithful to their calling even when it turns out that the One calling them is leading them not towards a pedestal, but an altar.

The Lord truly does give us *exceedingly abundantly above all that we ask or think,* but for our soul and our flesh this *exceedingly above* often turns out to be unexpectedly challenging, encroaching on the unbearable. The sacrifice of Isaac was the test that exceeded all Abraham could imagine, but along with it something *exceedingly abundantly above* what he could imagine was accomplished in his heart, and additionally at the end of the chapter the Lord gives him *exceedingly above* all he could ask or think as a reward. *'By Myself I have sworn, says the LORD, because you have done this thing, and have not withheld your son, your only son… in your seed all the nations of the earth shall be blessed, because you have obeyed My voice.'*[233] We will later revisit the promise God gave to Abraham as a reward for obedience, but for now let's rest in the knowledge that the Lord truly does reward and bless His chosen ones. He really has prepared for us a kingdom and priesthood, but the path to this priesthood, to this kingdom, differs greatly from that which we might *ask or think.*

✄ ✄ ✄

Is that all there is?

Thoughts such as those we have just spoken of often resurface when I get off a plane at Ben-Gurion Airport near Tel Aviv. "You can blindfold me and let me off a plane in ten different cities around the world and I will immediately identify Israel by the incredible spiritual tension which literally electrifies the air here to the point of sparks." These words, more or less, were spoken

---

[231] Mat. 26:39
[232] Mat. 20:16
[233] Gen. 22:16,18

many years ago by a preacher who was outstandingly dedicated to Israel, and described a time when life in our country was incomparably more peaceful than it is now. I remember these words every time upon returning home from abroad, invariably struggling during the first couple days back after returning from some other "normal", peaceful country. A trip abroad from Israel, say to Finland and back, is somewhat like taking a trip to the moon: you have not simply spent time in some other country inhabited by generally the same type of people who live just a slightly different lifestyle, but you have experienced a completely different way of life, a totally foreign existence that we have given up reaching for.

Especially tense during the first few days back, I look into the faces of my fellow citizens and ask, why? Why are we not allowed to simply live like all the rest? Why is what others consider a normal life so totally remote, such an impossibility, a dream that can never come true for us, the chosen ones? Exhausted by the non-stop wandering through this desert of affliction, countless wars and escalating terror, all we really want for ourselves is a normal, peaceful life. On days such as the one on which I am now writing – *Yom Hazikaron,* the Day of Remembrance for fallen soldiers and victims of terror – when considering the disproportionately high number of orphaned families, a tally almost impossible to fathom for a country as miniscule as ours, one can understand this desire for peace in a particularly heart-wrenching way. Yet even as we long for nothing more than a normal, peaceful life there is something else, something more, something *above all that we ask or think* that the Lord desires for us. As was already stated, His purposes for us are simply *exceedingly abundantly above* the plans we have for ourselves.

In the first chapter we spoke about how the earthly history of Israel is commonly regarded as punishment while in fact, similar to the case of Job, it is not punishment but election to a special, sacrificial service in the purposes of God. We were **chosen for a special place in His plan.** In the second chapter, from the story of Benjamin we discovered that **our earthly history is one of His plans, not His feelings,** and that whatever the circumstances may be, a horizontal slice of this history at any particular moment does not necessarily characterize His heart-attitude towards us. We have come to realize that our suffering is in no way a testimony to His abandonment or rejection of us; His love for Israel is unwavering, though frequently imperceptible to the natural eye. Now I will attempt to answer one of the most difficult questions that torments the Jewish mind: why does suffering have to be a part of our calling? Why have the Jewish people suffered so greatly in the past, and continue to suffer so terribly to this day?

My question, His answer

Those who hate me without a cause are more than the hairs of my head; they are mighty who would destroy me, being my enemies wrongfully; though I have stolen nothing, I still must restore it. [234] **Why?** Why has the history of Israel been one of incessant horror for the duration of the past two millenniums – a history of cries and moans, blood and smoke, truly a story of *fire and a knife*, accompanying our ascent to the altar? How do you explain to an Israeli whose only desire is to live a quiet life and raise his children in safety, and who is ready to give almost anything in exchange (the only possible explanation for the absurd attempts of the "peace process"), why not only the past history of the chosen people was one of endless suffering, but the current situation is still so horrendous in Israel? "Why?" I asked the Lord. "Why have the people You love, chose and called Your own been forced to face such unbelievable sorrows?"

I have already described how He Himself stopped me when in my book about Job I had planned so freely and shamelessly to share ready-made Christian recipes for Israel with "my countrymen according to the flesh." This was only the beginning of His working in my heart concerning Israel. Though I do not think He is finished yet, so much has already changed in my husband's and my views, which used to run solely along the

---

[234] Ps. 69:4

traditional lines of Christianity's historical attitude towards Israel. Years ago, the book about Job became the clearest revelation to me of how helpless any human effort is in the face of suffering and the sufferer, if the Spirit of God is not in it. All the words of human wisdom which quite possibly work under normal circumstances are exposed as unfruitful, dangerous, or even deadly in the face of the suffering into which only the One *who gives life to the dead*[235] has the power to enter. This is why I approached this new book in earnest only when I fully submitted to the revelation that no theology could penetrate the mystery of Israel, that no doctrinal theses work in the face of our frequently unbearable and almost always unexplained suffering, and that only the Lord Himself is able to answer our groans and questions by His Spirit.

Years before the current war began, during the so-called "peacetime" when the thunder of explosions was not heard in Israel every day but only every month, I began to call on the Lord. "Answer me! Explain to me why You remain silent! Why do You not intervene? Can You really look so calmly and with such indifference at the shreds of blown-up children's bodies, at the orphaned families, at the 'survivors' maimed for life? Don't You hurt when we are hurting?" Naturally, I knew all the traditional, theologically correct answers and could give long-winded explanations to anyone who might ask, but alone with Him I cried and begged Him for an answer. Something was definitely lacking in my understanding. I, who knew all the answers, lacked **His answer,** His tangible participation, His audible voice, **His living tears.** "Lord," I wept, "aren't You weeping, too?"

His sovereign hand

The Lord answered me, and I will describe in detail how He did because it was out of His answer, many years ago now, that this book began to take shape. The year was 1996 and in May we had

---

[235] Rom. 4:17

elections in Israel.[236] In the evening when the ballot-boxes were opened and the tallying began, it became evident that the leftist Labor party *Avodah,* which during the course of the past four years had chopped up and distributed Israel piece by piece and armed those who today are shooting at us, would be remaining in power. At around twelve o'clock my husband and I turned from the television where the divided screen plainly showed the jubilation at the Labor Party Headquarters and the downcast faces of the rightist *Likud* electorate. We brought a prayer for our country before the Lord and having suffered enough distress for one evening, went to bed. There was nothing more to wait for; the Labor Party's lead already seemed more than convincing and the result of the elections perfectly clear. All that was left for us was to trust in the God of Israel, taking comfort in the fact that He loved His people and His country not any less than we did.

We both awoke at the same instant about three o'clock in the morning, roused by an indistinct but intense impression, whether a spiritual wind or the gentle touch of a hand, I can't be sure. I knew that something must be happening somewhere – whether in the air, or in the heavens I couldn't tell, but something just as sure as it was invisible. As we were getting up, my husband remarked, "Look, my pillow is soaked for some reason. It looks like I was crying in my sleep, but I don't have any recollection of it." Aware that the ballot-counting would be continuing all night, we switched on the television without any particular hope, just curious to find out what was going on. The screen was still divided in half and on it we could see both party headquarters – but how they had changed! Over the *Avodah* Headquarters reigned undisguised confusion and dismay, while at the *Likud* Party Headquarters, near euphoria. I later heard

---

[236] Since this time we have had elections three times, and I write these lines but a few days before yet another election. We now have them approximately every two years instead of the standard four. In combination with the day-by-day deterioration of our terrorized lives, these elections evoke all the fewer emotions and expectations. We are left with depleted hopes in mankind, and Israel is approaching ever closer to that point where we will truly only be able to trust in Him alone. Today we pray for the elections, but we used to look forward to them then in the hopes of stopping this monstrous "peace process" that is in opposition to the things of God and only serves to increase the bloody toll which we have mourned almost daily for nearly the past three years.

testimonies from other believers who at about the same time felt a peculiar inclination and looking out the window, saw hosts of angels filling the skies over Israel. Something supernatural happened that night; the Lord Himself sovereignly intervened in the course of events. Although God naturally does not identify Himself with any particular political party, He did not allow *Avodah* to come to power, shamelessly ungodly and flagrantly opposing Him as they were. Whether the candidates themselves experienced something unusual during those hours or not I don't know, but doubtless even they recognized the direct hand of God at work. That night the victor Benjamin Netanyahu, in his first speech as Prime Minister, began with words from the prophet Zechariah: *not by might nor by power, but by My Spirit, says the LORD of hosts.*[237]

Living tears

Some time later, after yet another terrorist attack and yet another series of funerals (at that time this seemed to happen terribly frequently; today, after two and a half years of war, one understands that it was peace-time), I again asked the Lord, "Why do You remain silent, God of Israel? Almighty Lord, why do You not intervene and protect Your people? *Why should You be like a stranger in the land, and like a traveler who turns aside to tarry for a night? Why should You be like... a mighty one who cannot save?*[238] Are You really able to bear all this calmly? Do you really not hurt when we feel pain? Don't You cry when we do?"

Then, in answer to my tears and my cry, the Lord very simply and distinctly said to me, "**I am crying.** I also weep. Don't you remember those tears that night, that wet pillow? Don't you remember how your husband said that he must have been crying in his sleep and didn't know it? It was Me that night, crying through him. It was with My tears over Israel and

---

[237] Zech. 4:6
[238] Jer. 14:8-9

Jerusalem that his pillow was saturated. I wept that night – and I always weep together with you all."

From these tears – such real, such tangible, such **wet** tears shed by God – this book was born. The verse in Luke where Yeshua cries over Jerusalem – *as He drew near, He saw the city and wept over it*[239] – now spoke to my heart in a completely new way. Yes, I always knew that a few days before His suffering on the cross the Son of Man had wept not for Himself but for the cross-like suffering which lay ahead for His people, for the centuries of hatred and defamation, of Crusaders and the Inquisition, for the thousands who would die in pogroms and the millions doomed to disappear into the gas chambers. While I used to think that He was shedding tears two thousand years in advance in this verse, mourning all our future sufferings, now after the wet pillow incident (after my *hands have handled*[240] His tears), I know for certain that He weeps over Israel today in exactly the same way He did then. He hurts when we are hurting, our countless wounds are His open running wound, and the tears pouring from our eyes are His tears, as well.

Nothing can touch a heart more deeply than seeing God's tears. Nothing can equal witnessing the overflowing eyes of the One you considered to be indifferently responsible for all your sorrows, who is apparently causing or at least allowing you to suffer, the One to whom you had again and again addressed angry and accusing monologues. In the previous chapter, by His Holy Spirit the Lord displayed for us His **tears of love** through Joseph in *his chamber;* we saw God weeping but restraining His love for Israel. In this chapter He wants to show us His **tears of compassion**: the living, warm salty tears of Yeshua – tears visible not only to us but also to those who encountered Him during His earthly life.

I believe that one of the reasons the Lord has given me this book is for its readers to see **His tears and His compassion.** Could you be the one to whom He especially wants to speak through these

---

[239] Luke 19:41
[240] 1 John 1:1

words today? Perhaps it is your tattered and hardened heart He is seeking right now. If you are the one who for many years has turned and hidden from His gaze, the one who thought it impossible to be reconciled with God and forgive Him for the pain, the one who has accused Him over and over again for causing the suffering of Israel, a portion of which has become your personal suffering, then raise your swollen and reddened eyes and behold how **He is weeping.** I pray that the soul doubled over with pain would be washed and renewed with His tears. I pray that the bleeding heart, deeply touched by His pain, will allow Him to lean down and bind up its wounds. I pray that someone's attitude towards God and his relationship with Him will be forever changed when he sees Him in our mirror: the Father who, while making Israel captive to His plan of salvation for the nations, weeps out of love in the inner room, yet restrains the yearning of His heart and His mercies; and the Son who, knowing that He came not only for His own crucifixion but also for the crucifixion of His own people on that same cross, weeps openly over all the torment to be unleashed on Israel in His name.

An answer from the Lord

All this became but the beginning of His conversation with me. I returned again and again in my thoughts to that wet pillow, repeatedly pondering His reason for weeping that night. Did He really not know what would happen just a short time later – that He Himself would intervene and everything would immediately be made right? Why did He shed those tears? "Why did you weep, Lord?" I continued to ask, sensing that there was something more that He wanted to show me, something that I had to see and understand., The *secret things* that *belong to the Lord,* however, are revealed only according to His will and only when He Himself lays them out plainly before us. "Do you really not understand?" He asked me. "Think back – something like this has already happened before. Remember!" Astonished, I suddenly did "remember": by the Holy Spirit He quickened to me one more gospel story with tears, a story where Yeshua wept barely a few moments before His own intervention in it.

You have probably guessed what I am referring to. If not, you need only to peek back at the verses introducing this chapter. In John's Gospel, standing at the grave of Lazarus, Yeshua weeps over the suffering and death of a person who in just a few moments He would raise from the dead. Of course I immediately lunged for my Bible and devoured these pages. Reading and rereading them, I began to make out a picture which though vague and sketchy at first, gradually started to emerge more and more distinctly before my inner gaze. Then, continuing the conversation, He asked, "And do you remember how many times Yeshua weeps in the Gospels?" Immediately I recognized the totally obvious fact that I had never before considered: in the entire New Testament, Yeshua weeps just twice – once over Jerusalem, and once over Lazarus. Suddenly, for the first time these two stories united against the backdrop of my internal screen. I am sure you have also experienced what I did at that moment – in one split second the Lord makes something you had never seen before as plain as day. It was as if for a long time something just hadn't fit and then finally, it fell into place all on its own, into the vacant spot prepared just for it. Something inside me went "click", confirming the revelation. I didn't know why that as far as I knew, no one had ever placed these two scenes side by side before. Of course after God reveals something it always seems so obvious, but in any case it was His desire that they be paired together for me. In answer to my prayers and meditations on His tears for Jerusalem, He purposefully showed me His tears just a few seconds before His own intervention in the events of the election so that I could remember His tears over Lazarus.

This was not the first time the Lord had used rather unusual ways to reveal His Word to me. For instance, I remember one occasion when, while praying, I ineptly reached for my Bible that was laying quite a distance away. In the process I fell down and knocked my knee really hard against something. It was so painful that when I finally got back up to get my Bible, I found myself limping rather clumsily. When I limped back and opened the Scriptures, I was astounded by what I read: *I will make the lame a remnant...*[241] In this startling way He answered my prayer regarding Israel and His perspective on my place within Israel.

To return to our topic, this was how I finally understood what the Lord was trying to tell me! The entire affair with His tears and the wet pillow that night had been designed for me to remember the story of Lazarus, through which He wanted to speak to me concerning Israel. Through my questions about His tears right before His intervention in the course of events, He reminded me about the story of Lazarus. Again, just like in a children's magazine where two pictures are placed side by side and one must find either the similarities or differences, He placed before my mind's eye these two scenes of His tears: tears over Jerusalem, and tears over Lazarus. The Lazarus story was revealed as an additional key to understanding the mystery of Israel or more precisely, as one more leaf of the mirror in which our fate and election were reflected at a new angle, with a new, piercing clarity.

"You ask Me what Israel is chosen for? I will show you what election means. I will show you a man chosen by God: chosen in order to glorify the Lord with an amazing miracle during Yeshua's earthly life – but also chosen to experience pain, to suffer, to toss and turn from fever and cry out with pain, to wait for the Lord and unable to wait any longer, to die and be placed in the grave. He was chosen so that his suffering would be so great that the Son of God, before being glorified through his suffering, wept over him – just as He wept over Jerusalem before being glorified in her. He was chosen in order to undergo suffering *exceedingly abundantly above* what he could think in order to obtain a resultant blessing that was exceedingly abundantly above what he could imagine. He was chosen for suffering, but this suffering became only the prologue to the glory of God, the purpose for which, in essence, he was destined."

---

[241] Mic. 4:7

Through the tears of Yeshua, the Lord helped me to see the election of Israel reflected in the election of Lazarus and this became His answer to my tears, His response to all my questions. Although much of Israel's earthly path is unclear to us, being yet sealed, in this gospel story Yeshua explains in detail to His disciples (and to us) the purpose and design for what is happening. Israel, reflected in Lazarus, can therefore be perceived in a completely different light, from a view-point much closer to God's. In this chapter we will speak of Lazarus and his election, and of course about Israel and their election. Let's start at the very beginning of our Scripture passage, John chapter eleven: *now a certain man was sick, Lazarus of Bethany.*[242]

⚬ ⚬ ⚬

Only the beginning

Now a certain man was sick, Lazarus of Bethany. The chapter begins in this simple, prosaic way, with the several agonizing days of sickness almost imperceptibly concentrated in this one short sentence. Over the course of several hours Lazarus' seemingly not-so-serious indisposition develops into a dangerous illness, with his fever, pain and delirium feeding the growing alarm of the sisters, but the passage is constructed in such a way as to keep everything that happened to Lazarus outside the view of the reader. The complete drama of Bethany is hidden from us and though by all means part of His plan, we later find it was only the preface to this plan.

In contrast to the Book of Job, almost all of which we wait in wearied expectancy for the final chapters where the Lord Himself intervenes in the story, the entire chapter of John eleven is dedicated to Yeshua's arrival at Bethany. The days of sickness, suffering and waiting are compressed into a few lines; as is typical, nothing in the Scriptures tells us about the perplexed feelings of those who were waiting. To a great extent, Job's

---

[242] John 11:1

overwhelming pain, bewilderment, and resentment against God make up the text of the Book of Job; these same emotions which doubtless filled Lazarus and his sisters remain between the lines of John chapter eleven. Moreover, if we experience Job's story of suffering and sadness through the eyes of Job himself, then in Lazarus' story of suffering, sadness, death and resurrection, we hear not a sound – not a question, groan or cry – from Lazarus himself, just as we hear not a word out of Benjamin. Lazarus and his sufferings pass by the readers almost unnoticed, and one might think that they had almost passed unnoticed by Yeshua as well, if it were not for His tears at the grave which we will soon discuss. This story is witnessed by outsiders and presented to us exclusively through them. In contrast to the Book of Job, where *the LORD answered Job out of the whirlwind,*[243]even all of the Lord's commentary and explanations are addressed not to Lazarus but to others: to the disciples, the sisters, and the by-standers.

Naturally all of this is not simply chance, for there is nothing inadvertent about the Word of God; each of these Scriptures answers its own question and fulfills its own task. The Book of Job answers the cries and questions of the suffering Job: you are not being punished, you were chosen for suffering and through this suffering your heart will be reborn. Similar to Job, Lazarus is not being punished; he was chosen for suffering. In this case, however, the Lord chose him for suffering primarily so that the **hearts of others** could be transformed and reborn. Although we can assume that the comforters in the Book of Job also experience repentance and renewal in the end, God relates the story of Job to us mainly in connection with the person of Job himself, and everything that happens with his friends is in one way or another secondary. In the story of Lazarus, on the other hand, his sickness, death and resurrection were recorded by the Lord primarily so that we could view God's election in action: **one chosen to suffer for the sake of others** (though again, I do not have the tiniest doubt that Lazarus' resurrection was not limited to the physical sense and that he also came forth from the

---

[243] Job 40:6

grave reborn spiritually). This is why this story is such an important key to understanding the destiny of Israel.

A ray of hope

The second verse of our chapter is intriguing. In specifying the identities of Mary and Martha, Lazarus' sisters, the Gospel writer confirms that Mary was the one *who anointed the Lord with fragrant oil and wiped His feet with her hair.*[244] This comment might go almost undetected except for one small detail: Mary *anointed the feet of Jesus, and wiped His feet with her hair*[245] only after the resurrection of Lazarus, in the following twelfth chapter of John. At this moment, at the beginning of Lazarus' sickness, those who are reading the Gospel in order chapter by chapter have not yet met his sisters and therefore cannot know anything about them.[246] It is my belief that the Gospel writer's apparent "mistake" was fully intentional; it is as if from the very beginning of the story, the Author of the Word inserted a secret passageway, indicative of a hidden hope that connects the story with the future. Those who know God's handwriting will agree that such a feature is highly characteristic of Him. With the advent of these terrible days, it begins to seem to Lazarus and his sisters that all of life with the Lord, His relationship with them, their faithfulness to Him, His love for them, everything that He taught them and everything they learned, is left on the other side of the dividing line that now separates their lives into two segments of before and after: *now a certain man was sick, Lazarus of Bethany.*[247] Yes, Lazarus is sick and as far as we know, he gets worse and worse. No comforting signs appear, hopes fade and faith weakens, but in this seemingly impenetrable darkness the Lord leaves us a ray of His light, and the ostensibly pitch-black and hopeless present is transformed, lit up by this ray of light pointing to the future. The sensitive reader, having

---

[244] John 11:2
[245] John 12:3
[246] The famous episode with the sisters, '*Martha, Martha, you are worried and troubled about many things,*' is found in the Gospel of Luke, chapter ten.
[247] John 11:1

followed this faint marker, will flip ahead to the twelfth chapter and from there return to the eleventh assured that however gloomy and dark the day appeared to Lazarus and his sisters, another day was also certain to dawn in their lives.

While all of this does not bear a direct relation to the theme of this book or this chapter, for some reason the Lord has laid these thoughts on my heart. Perhaps they will be significant to someone reading these pages. No, we are not allowed to hurry forward through the pages of our life and peek into the next chapter; nevertheless, the Lord wants us to be able to identify these hidden signs of His love which link us to the future. He wants us to see His guiding arrow in the text of our lives that leads us on to brighter days. No matter how grim the darkness is that surrounds us now, no matter how gloomy and threatening your circumstances are today, believe me when I say that His light shines even in such darkness. The seedling of hope which you can't yet see, or perhaps which you don't even care to see but which pierces through the darkness and pain, is gradually but definitely budding somewhere in your heart, pushing its way up to get through to the light. Do not fear the risk of increased pain, do not uproot this small shoot, this trembling green branch that is forcing its way through the stone tiles forged by your heart, but open up to the Lord. Allow His love and gentleness to touch your wounded soul and bring life to what you thought was dead. Allow the story of Lazarus to become your story as well; allow the One *who gives life to the dead*[248] to come and raise you up!

He whom You love

Coming to the third verse, we find Mary and Martha so alarmed that they finally resolve to trouble their beloved Teacher. The words they use to inform Yeshua of their brother Lazarus' sickness are surprising: *'Lord, behold, he whom You love is sick.'*[249]

---

[248] Rom. 4:17
[249] John 11:3

Let's take some time to meditate on the text of this brief message. Yeshua who came to earth because *God so loved the world*[250] was the incarnation of the Father's love – the Word of love, sent to the earth with a heart of love – and I think it is safe to say that this love was experienced by each one with whom He came in contact. Disturbed, we might ask: where did they get such self-confidence? How could they be so arrogant? Did not Yeshua love everyone else, too? Did the sisters have the right to so elevate Lazarus over others, and to so emphasize the special love the Lord had for him? I am inclined to think that at this moment they were not especially concerned about the theological accurateness of their message, or about justifying its implications; they were just in a hurry to inform Yeshua that their brother was sick, and had searched out the most brief, clear, and precise formulation for this message. Paradoxically, these surprising words, the one *whom You love,* seemed to Lazarus' sisters the most meaningful and specific ones that would denote their brother even more directly than mentioning his name. To all appearances, Yeshua was connected with him in such a special way, so precious was Lazarus in His eyes, so great was His love for him, that not only for Lazarus' sisters, but for the Lord Himself the phrase *behold, he whom You love* was a perfectly simple and yet exhaustive description of the patient.

Not once in my life have I ever heard even a fragment of a message preached on these words. It seems uncomfortable for preachers to speak about how the Lord, while loving everybody, could have a special love for someone. To me, however, these words are priceless: God's special relationship to our people shines though them, and indeed through the entire story of Lazarus. God who *so loved the world*[251] does love each one of us, irrespective of nationality or country of residence, and yet the exquisitely tender words recorded in Jeremiah that still speak to hearts today, *'I have loved you with an everlasting love,'*[252] were originally addressed to Israel and remain God's declaration of love for His people. I believe our Lord would have immediately

---

[250] John 3:16
[251] John 3:16
[252] Jer. 31:3

grasped the underlying meaning of the words in the sisters' message: *he whom You love...*[253] Through this brief note of entreaty or this prayer, essentially, which the sisters dispatch to Yeshua, the Lord is teaching believers how to properly pray for His people.

Years ago I was acquainted with an elderly Estonian sister whose heart was filled with an enormous love for Israel. Similar to Anna the prophetess in the Gospel of Luke, who *served God with fastings and prayers night and day,*[254] she persistently interceded before God for the chosen people. She is now with the Lord so I cannot inquire as to what specific words she used when she prayed, but I believe that the essence of her prayers was this: *'Lord, behold he whom You love is sick.'* Not, "Lord, behold the one you rejected and punished is sick," not, "Lord, behold the one who sinned is sick," the haughty and condescending way people frequently pray for Israel but rather, *'Lord, behold he whom You love is sick'* – Your beloved is in pain, he is hurting. This is the only correct text for you, in the place of Lazarus' sisters, to use in speaking to God about Israel. In your deepest heart you must know not only that this people is sorrowful, suffering and longing for God's healing, but also that God has loved them with a special, eternal love that He will never renounce. If this seems theologically unjustifiable to you ("Why would God single out any one person or people?"), if even for a second you stumble over this election, if any feeling slightly akin to jealousy or resentment darkens your heart, then remember that the *one whom [He] loves* **is sick.** Remember that for Lazarus, his Lord's special love for him was accompanied first and foremost by sickness and sorrow, suffering and death, and finally by being laid in the grave. Israel's election is that of Lazarus: the Lord's special love and unique plan for us, shadowed in the story of Lazarus, is one that also encompasses pain, torment, suffering and being "abandoned" by God. Resurrection is unavoidably preceded by dying – are you truly ready to envy an election that so resembles a cross?

---

[253] John 11:3
[254] Luke 2:37

For the glory of God

So as we have seen, Lazarus was special in the eyes of the Lord. Lazarus' sickness, evidently, was also seen by Him as unusual and special because having been informed of it, Yeshua says, *'This sickness is not unto death, but for the glory of God, that the Son of God may be glorified through it.'*[255] A heart which is sensitive to the Word of God and a spirit which is open to His Spirit is sure to recognize God's tell-tale handwriting. Promises such as these, which assure us of a revelation of God's glory at the end of all suffering, are given to Israel numerous times in the *Tenach*. This is the reason that the Lord uses the story of Lazarus to illustrate the way this glory is achieved. Before becoming a story of God's glory, it must first be one of sickness, suffering and death. *'Most assuredly, I say to you, unless a grain of wheat falls into the ground and dies...'*[256]

We are told at the outset that not only Lazarus is special to Yeshua, but his sickness is also special; it is defined from the beginning as being *for the glory of God*. As soon as Yeshua learns of this sickness, wouldn't it be natural for Him to drop everything and hurry to heal Lazarus? But this isn't how it happens in the Gospel account! I assume that my readers know the story of Lazarus quite well, so I will not weary you with drawn-out dramatic pauses. Yes, there is nothing we can do about it. In the place where each one of us would like to read, "When He heard that Lazarus was sick, He made haste to heal him," instead we find something altogether different. *So, when He heard that he was sick, He stayed two more days in the place where He was.*[257]

In preaching from this chapter, almost no one can withstand the temptation to describe these emotionally charged days: Lazarus tossing from fever, the sisters taking turns keeping watch at his bedside, the frustrated expectancy, hope turning to despair.

---

[255] John 11:4
[256] John 12:24
[257] John 11:6

Then finally it is all over. Lazarus has died and Yeshua never showed up. But as I consider these days, it seems to me that the most difficult thing would not be the waiting, but the bewildering incomprehension: why, why does He not come? I can imagine Mary and Martha, trying and utterly failing to grasp what is going on and why the Lord has deserted them. I can imagine Lazarus, coming to himself from time to time, asking through dried, cracked lips, "He hasn't come yet?" and again sinking into unconsciousness. The Scriptures do not describe the feelings of the patient, but judging by what the sisters say to Yeshua when He finally arrives in Bethany, I can guess that it was extremely difficult for Lazarus to continue to believe, and that his last days were filled with the bitterness and pain resulting from his imagined rejection.

Even more distinctly than Lazarus and his sisters, however, I can picture their neighbors, surveying the whole bitter drama from their windows and shaking their heads in wonder. "He still hasn't come! We had thought that He loved him, but it looks like He's not going to come. He probably has more important business to attend to. He must not love Lazarus all that much. Maybe Lazarus has sinned and Yeshua is disappointed in him, and so has forgotten and left him. Maybe He never really did love him." I can visualize such talk floating around Bethany during those days and finally breaking the hearts of the sisters. Could the Lord really have abandoned their brother? Had Yeshua really stopped loving Lazarus? Did their suffering mean nothing to the One, of whose love they had been so confident just a few days back, when they had sent the messenger to Him?

As we are plunged into the midst of this drama, we again become witnesses of the same striking feature we found in the stories of Job and Joseph. This entire book has developed out of the marvelous signature left by the Author on these Biblical texts. Just as in those other stories, there is a secret in the story of Lazarus which is completely hidden from the story's participants until just the right time. It is the secret of **God's love** (*now Jesus loved Martha and her sister and Lazarus[258]*), which is **hidden within God's plan** (*'this sickness is not unto death, but for the glory of God'[259]*). Neither Lazarus or his sisters, nor those near them during these terrible days, naturally, could have heard Yeshua's words regarding the purpose of Lazarus' sickness. Likewise, they did not have the opportunity to read the author's commentary about His love for them, just as Job did not read the prologue to his book, nor Benjamin see Joseph's tears in the inner room. However, just as in the stories of Job and Benjamin, you and I know from the very beginning that **the Lord loves Lazarus.** How different, then, is the perspective of the one who authoritatively knows about this love hidden from the participants, from that of the participants themselves! Those acquainted with the Prologue to Job do not suspect God of punishing the righteous man chosen and beloved by Him. Those who witness Joseph crying in the inner room do not doubt his love for Benjamin, even when he puts the cup into the sack of his unsuspecting brother. Similarly, no matter what happens to Lazarus in the rest of the story, since you and I have been told with all certainty, with all the credibility of the Word of God, that Yeshua loves Lazarus, we perceive Yeshua's actions, His entire plan concerning Lazarus, in the light of the unquestionable and absolutely reliable love of God.

Faith, against all odds

If you will, this is a lesson for every believer. In our real-time lives we frequently find ourselves in Lazarus' shoes, where the fourth and fifth verses of the chapter, i.e. the author's comments intended for the reader concerning God's love and plan, are hidden from us in exactly the same way they were hidden from Lazarus. Upon finding ourselves in some strange and difficult situation, we are habitually inclined towards initial confidence that any minute now the Lord will intervene and make everything turn out all right. We expect His arrival any minute,

---

[258] John 11:5
[259] John 11:4

but time goes by and the circumstance only worsens; the Lord remains silent, doesn't show Himself, and we gradually begin to doubt the veracity of His love... Where are You, Lord? I put so much trust in You, I believed in You, why are You so quiet? Can it be true that You don't love me, could You really have forgotten me? Does my suffering mean nothing to You? Aren't you coming to help me, to save me, to heal me? The eleventh chapter of John teaches us that however tragic or inexplicable the current circumstances we find ourselves in seem to be, they are not accidental. Just as in the story of Lazarus, the secrets of God's love and His plan are concealed at their core.

Now faith is the substance of things hoped for, the evidence of things not seen,[260] states the Word of God. In the stories the Lord revealed to me for inclusion in this book, God's love turns out to be the secret ingredient that remains invisible due to the tragic visible circumstances. Ultimately, all this can be summed up in a simple, almost banal assertion which despite its triteness is nonetheless enormously difficult for believers to walk out: **faith is continuing to believe in God's love even when everything around us testifies to the opposite**. Despite all odds, press on to obtain a faith such as this. Focus your trust on the One who created you. Strive to possess a confidence in His love for you, even if neither you nor others can see this love right now. Remember that even if His plan hides His love from you, in fact it is on this love that His plan has been based. It is through such plans that the Lord is truly preparing us for the priesthood and for the kingdom. He does genuinely desire to give us *exceedingly abundantly above all that we ask or think,*[261] but it is down His path and not ours that He leads us towards what is *exceedingly abundantly above.*

❊ ❊ ❊

---

[260] Heb. 11:1
[261] Eph. 3:20

Israel's identity crisis

We have seen how prior to his sickness, Lazarus was absolutely confident of Yeshua's love for him. He knew that he was beloved of the Lord and that the Lord would not leave him. This brings us back to our discussion of Israel. Just as in Lazarus' story, up until the very time Yeshua came into the world (or more precisely, until the rise of Christianity), Israel was fully confident in the knowledge that they were a special, peculiar people belonging to God. It was not because of our pride, but because of His living Word that we knew our people were the ones whom He loves. This definition of Lazarus that the sisters found for the message to Yeshua, *the one whom You love,* in essence was the national identity of Israel, ingrained in them by God Himself.

The changes which took place two thousand years ago, from Israel's standpoint, are understood only with the greatest of difficulty, just as Lazarus could not understand what was going on during the final few days of his illness. At least from the perspective of traditional Christian theology, the God of Israel was seen as abandoning His people: into the world He sends His Messiah, so long expected by the oppressed Israel (and expected by no one else, incidentally), but unexpectedly in conjunction with this, the heavenly riches of mercy and grace are instead poured out on the descendants of other nations and Israel is condemned to centuries-long suffering. Is this fathomable? Could God really "betray" His people? Could He really act this way toward the ones whom He had called His beloved son and firstborn?

When I was yet a young believer, I heard a message by a preacher who, in describing the Father's sacrifice and Yeshua's death on the cross, used his own son in an illustration. "I have a young son," he said. "He's a timid, shy boy who is easily frightened and loves me, his father, very much. Imagine that one of my acquaintances were to commit some crime, was convicted and given the death penalty. Imagine that I decided to redeem his life at the price of the life of my son. Settling the arrangements with the rather surprised but finally approving judge, I come home and tell my son, 'Come here, let's go. I have something I need you to do.' His trust of me is perfect and he follows me without questions or suspicion. Together we go to the prison where he is slated to die. It is dark and scary there and I see how frightened he is, how he looks at me, seeking support and comfort in my eyes, seeing in me the assurance that nothing bad is going to happen to him. My heart is breaking, but turning my eyes from him, eternally dear and horribly fearful, with a nod of my head I give the sign to begin. The last thing I see is the eyes of my son concentrated on me and filled with terror and incomprehension. 'What are you doing to me, Dad?' his eyes literally cry out – and then all is over. Shaken by sobs, I run away from that horrible room."

Of course, that was not the end of the message. The preacher spoke about how this father must have felt if the person whose freedom he had purchased at the unbearably high price of his own son, in leaving the prison, didn't even bother to thank him and only laughed in his face. This is how those who do not accept the sacrifice of Golgotha are behaving – such was the point of this frightening illustration. But years later the Lord brought it back to my memory in speaking with me about His son Israel. I wrote in the Prologue that the difference between Yeshua and Isaac was that Yeshua fully understood for what purpose He *came to this hour*,[262] while Isaac did not have any idea about where the father was leading him and what he intended to do with him. The image of the son, infinitely trusting his father and being led by him to his death, is etched into my memory and fits perfectly both our understanding of Isaac and what we are reading in the story of Lazarus. It is an apt illustration of what the Lord has shown me about Israel.

It is impossible to describe the emotions experienced by a person when the one of whose love he is absolutely confident treats him in seeming discordance with this love. Lazarus was confident of Yeshua's love and expected Him at any minute, but Yeshua still didn't come. For him these few torturous days of illness became the contradiction to all that he knew about the Lord, the

---

[262] John 12:27

inconsistency that refuted the entire experience of that relationship. Continuing the parallel between Lazarus and Israel, we can say that the events of the first century became just such a completely unexpected and unfeasibly horrifying obstacle to Israel's comprehension. The people who had been completely confident of the Lord's love for them and their special meaning and election in Him were ridiculed and despised, nearly obliterated. The Temple was destroyed, and tens of thousands of Jewish people were killed and taken into captivity. Moreover, in one voice with this horrible reality, as if mocking our election, the Gentile Christians began to say that Israel had been punished and abandoned by God, that they had forfeited their election and ceased from being the people of God, that God had rejected Israel and now loved only the Church.

This whole time, the Lord remained silent and allowed all this to happen. Every expectation of Israel, similar to that of Lazarus that He would even now intervene, would demonstratively prove His love, would protect and justify His own, proved in vain. It was as if the Heavenly Father Himself had taken his beloved, trusting son by the hand and led him down a path of suffering and sacrifice, as illustrated by the heart-rending example of the father and son from that long-ago message. The mercy, grace and light of the living God of Israel turned out to be intended for others while Israel, bewildered, shaken, and not comprehending, ended up being led by His hand into darkness. In this sense our history bears a remarkable resemblance to the story of Lazarus. In one moment everything unexpectedly changed for him, and in just a few days of sickness he went from being a beloved friend, completely secure in his close relationship to the Lord and assured of His love, to being abandoned and rejected, at least in the eyes of others. This is the exact way the situation changed so unexpectedly for Israel. Without warning or readily available explanation, in the eyes of decidedly all who surrounded them, they went from being a beloved, chosen people to a people abandoned and rejected, a nation of outcasts.

Did Israel succeed in clinging to their belief that God loved them and that they remained the chosen people in His eyes, despite their ceaseless affliction and the apparent silence of the Lord? Think back to that heart-rending cry of Jeremiah: *'Why should You be... like a mighty one who cannot save?'* Immediately following this verse, the prophet utters these amazing words by the inspiration of the Holy Spirit: *'Yet You, O LORD, are in our midst, and we are called by Your name.'*[263] Only the true presence of God in the midst of His people, a presence even more certain and more real than their oh-so-tangible pain and anguish, can explain this faith that has continued to live on in our hearts, faith that says the Lord is among us and with us even when He remains silent. *We are called by His name* even when He is *like a mighty one who cannot save.* Despite tremendous odds, Israel persisted. They continued to love a God who silently permitted all their suffering and kept on believing in both His love for them and their special status as the "chosen people".

Two more days

This *evidence of things not seen,* this confidence in the hearts of Israel of His love and their election, was sustained by the Lord Himself and was the thing that gave them the power to survive. He was the One who fed the hope that helped Israel remain an identifiable people group, though scattered. Furthermore, when we read, *He stayed two more days in the place where He was,* one can't help but remember that it has been exactly two millenniums since the time this took place, since Israel was last taken into captivity, by sickness and suffering, as it were. For the extent of two full millenniums, our people have lived under the perpetual accusation that God is not coming for us but has abandoned us. The Scriptures tell us, however, that *with the Lord one day is as a thousand years, and a thousand years as one day.*[264] This is why with all my heart I believe that the "two days" of Lazarus' story are drawing to a close and soon the time will

---

[263] Jer. 14:9
[264] 2 Pet. 3:8

come when the Lord says to his disciples, *'Let us go to Judea again.'*[265]

Remember how Isaiah puts it: *Listen! Your watchmen lift up their voices; together they shout for joy.* **When the LORD returns to Zion, they will see it with their own eyes.**[266] I have already mentioned that the verse that strikes me as one of the most agonizing, the most tragic in all the New Testament is Luke chapter four, verse thirty, which describes how Yeshua went out from among his angered countrymen. *Then passing through the midst of them, He went His way.* What an overwhelming sense of comfort it is for us, Israeli believers, to now hear the words of the Lord directed at His disciples: *'Let us go to Judea again.'* Only the watchmen of Israel, those whose hearts are pained and whose souls are in agony over the suffering of His people, only those who do not remain silent before Him but day and night intercede for Israel – *'Lord, behold, he whom You love is sick'* – only they can fully appreciate the overwhelming joy captured in these words: *'Let us go to Judea again.'* **The Lord is returning to Zion!**

Love restrained

This whole book began with the revelation about Lazarus, and I originally thought to have the story of Lazarus become the first chapter. However, the Lord intervened and changed the order of the chapters so that upon reaching this point, we who have learned to see the Lord in His *chamber* would already understand that no matter how difficult these days prior to Yeshua's arrival were for Lazarus, and no matter how difficult they were for Mary and Martha, they were much more difficult for Him! We know the love Yeshua had for Lazarus and his sisters. Imagine you have just been informed that someone very dear to you is extremely ill and about to die, and you are not with him. Moreover, you have no way of getting to him and there is

---

[265] John 11:7
[266] Is. 52:8 (NIV)

nothing you can do for him. I am sure that these days would be hard for you as well. Without a doubt, these days were difficult for Him, and again we ask ourselves the question: why did He not go immediately? Why did he condemn Lazarus and his sisters, and indeed Himself, to this suffering? Was not He, the omnipotent God, free to do what He wanted? Could not the Lord who loved Lazarus deliver him from these sufferings? *'Could not this Man, who opened the eyes of the blind, also have kept this man from dying?'*[267]

In the last chapter we spoke about the restrained love of the Lord, and about how for the sake of His plan He is often obliged to withhold and restrain His mercy towards the one He loves. The story of Lazarus is yet another exquisitely beautiful and profound illustration of this spiritual principle we are endeavoring to grasp. The Lord *restrained* **His love** for Lazarus and did not go to him (and now we can understand that He also suffered in doing so) in order for **His plan** to be accomplished through this story – so that this sickness would truly be to His glory! Just as in the stories of Job and Joseph, however, none of the people actually participating in the events were able to see this plan ahead of time or understand the true reason for what was going on. They were kept from knowing the Lord's real feelings until the story's conclusion.

When Yeshua finally comes, by this time Lazarus *had already been in the tomb four days*,[268] and Mary and Martha, making almost no attempt to hide their disappointment, each say exactly the same thing. *'Lord, if You had been here, my brother would not have died.'*[269] The entirety of the immense pain these horrible days caused is compressed into the bitterness of these few words which, try as they might not to reproach, yet reproach all the same: why, why were You not here, Lord? Why did You not come? Why did you leave us in this sorrow? How could it possibly be that You didn't love him? But then, right in front of those same neighbors, who had been whispering all these days that He had given up loving

---

[267] John 11:37
[268] John 11:17
[269] John 11:21,32

Lazarus and had abandoned him, deciding that this was the reason He hadn't come – before their very eyes something utterly remarkable happens, something inconsistent with their evaluations and theories. *Jesus wept.*[270]

In the Word of God there are no accidents or random flukes. If it was important to the Spirit of God to preserve the words *Jesus wept* in the Gospel text, then something altogether vital is being conveyed to the readers by these words. But what? Why, oh why, did He weep? Why did He cry over Lazarus? Didn't He know that in just a few moments a great miracle would take place, that He Himself would raise Lazarus from the dead and that Lazarus, alive, would come forth from the tomb? Of course the Lord knew, but why then did He weep?

The evidence of love

For me, the most glorious thing about these tears is their total inconsistency with what has happened in the part of the story visible to the participants up until now. Not only do they not support the judgments of the neighbors who saw Lazarus as abandoned and rejected, but neither do they confirm the bitter suspicion of the offended sisters. In addition, they do not appear to match up with the fact of His non-arrival itself, His fatal delay. They somehow do not fit with the events of Bethany up to this point, and represent the same type of contrast to visible reality as Joseph's *chamber* contrasted with what he did to his brothers outwardly. We even find words here reminiscent of the inner room: *then Jesus, again groaning in Himself, came to the tomb.*[271] Yeshua's tears at this point, from the perspective of the outward scene, at first appear almost excessive or unnecessary (why weep if Lazarus is just about to be raised from the dead anyway?) and just as in the story of Joseph, the Lord records them here only for the purpose of showing us His inner feelings, His heart.

---

[270] John 11:35
[271] John 11:38

Yeshua led Lazarus through this suffering with His own hand. Today when we witness these tears in the text, we are able to recognize that all this time He suffered together with Lazarus, just as the people who stood near Him then were able to recognize. We (not Lazarus) are of course informed from the beginning that *'this sickness is not unto death, but for the glory of God,'*[272] and that Lazarus was chosen to glorify the Lord through his suffering. Consequently, from the outset you and I (again, not Lazarus) realize that this sickness and death is all part of His plan. However, it was still extremely important to the Author to show just how difficult all this was for the Lord Himself and how much pain Lazarus' suffering caused Him, what grief the distress of His friend gave Him despite the fact that He had personally designed Lazarus' pain and distress. The truth of His love for Lazarus was demonstrated so clearly at this moment that while the people assembled by the tomb most likely included those neighbors who had recently passed judgment on Lazarus and considered him to be abandoned by the Lord, they had only one thing to say about those tears. Touched to the bottom of their hearts by the evidence of His love for Lazarus, they were able only to utter these words: *'See how He loved him!'*[273]

The path to glory

Essentially, the entire chapter of John eleven presents a two-fold lesson on Israel. First of all, Lazarus' story teaches us that everything that has been happening to Israel was planned by God from the very beginning and that He Himself is the Author of this story. With His temporary "rejection" of the people of Israel, God was in fact choosing them for the greatest of miracles and to bring Him great glory: *'I have created [you] for My glory.'*[274] Our path to this glory, however, is similar to the path of Lazarus, which lies through sacrifice and suffering. This is the objective

---

[272] John 11:4
[273] John 11:36
[274] Is. 43:7

side of His plan, but the Scriptures go even further to show us an inner, subjective (if one can say such a thing about God) side of this plan; we see how He *groans* inwardly together with us, we see how many tears and how much pain and sorrow that Israel's tears, pain and sorrow cause Him. The Lord who loves His people so infinitely suffers together with us, and this is in spite of the fact that our suffering is a part of His plan for us. At Lazarus' tomb Yeshua cries over the pain through which He has had to take Lazarus during those days of sickness and failed expectations, over the torture of incomprehension that filled his final hours and over how it had *already been... four days*[275] since he was laid in the tomb.

Yeshua weeps over Jerusalem with the same tears of love and compassion that He wept over Lazarus. "See how He loves him" can be our only response. He cries for the suffering through which God would have to take His people, about the torture of waiting for the Lord and the inability to comprehend why He remains silent while their hearts would be broken during the pogroms, the Inquisition and the Holocaust. He weeps that such is His plan, and that with His own hand He Himself will for long centuries lead Israel into the darkness of sickness and rejection. Although our Lord knows that in a few moments' time Lazarus will be raised, He weeps at the tomb of Lazarus over the pain of His beloved and over the path to this resurrection. He weeps over Jerusalem in this exact way. Though He knows that in just a few "moments" *(with the Lord...a thousand years [is] as one day)*[276] Jerusalem will burst forth from her captivity, He mourns the boundless suffering His beloved must endure on the path to resurrection.

[275] John 11:17
[276] 2 Pet. 3:8

When realities collide

Do you remember that *faith is... the evidence of things not seen?* Everything we read in the story of Lazarus up until the tears of Yeshua is the observable part of God's plan, and we have already discovered in the previous chapters that the part of His plan that is visible at any specific moment, despite what the witnesses or participants in the events themselves may think, frequently bears no resemblance to His actual feelings. We have come to understand through our various heroes that everything happening to them, while at first glance seeming to testify undeniably to their abandonment, was in fact sourced in a wonderfully tender and brightly burning love which was simply invisible to them at that moment. This is what must be said concerning Israel.

We have already discussed how the Church declared the tragic visible circumstances of our earthly history as the evidence that God had rejected His people. The principle of faith, *the substance of things hoped for, the evidence of things not seen* – this confidence in the invisible love of God did not function for the Christian world when it came to Israel. The reason the Lord called this book into existence was so that we could really see His unchanging though often unseen love for His people, concealed behind the façade of Israel's visible history. He wants those who are accustomed to judging by outward circumstances and who notice only the cup in the bag or the unhealed illness to look upon His tears of love and compassion in the inner room. He is revealing for us things invisible to the world through the reflections of these biblical stories.

We are approaching the moment in Lazarus' story where the invisible begins to shine through the visible, where the narrative crosses over for the first time from the level of the outer crust of the circumstances to the level of the veiled inner workings. The words *Jesus wept,* as I have already said, represent a truly astounding contrast between everything that had happened up until then because they revealed a new, as-of-yet invisible reality, **the reality of God's heart and God's love.** In verse thirty-eight we witness the first moment that these two realities, the inner and outer, collide and clash with each other. The extraordinarily substantial, extremely valid, the immoveable, irrefutable, stony-faced (both literally and figuratively) reality tempts us to see the inner reality of His love for Lazarus and His sorrow over him as inconsequential and impotent compared to the visible facts: *the tomb... was a cave, and a stone lay against it.*[277]

Let's stop for a minute and take a look back. Just a few days ago there lived a man in Bethany that everyone, himself included, knew was close to Yeshua and knew that Yeshua loved him. Lazarus had met with the Lord many times, listened to His messages and doubtless belonged to the followers and believers in Yeshua. Loving Yeshua and whole-heartedly devoted to Him, Lazarus did not doubt that he was beloved. Having fallen ill, at first he wouldn't even have been worried; rather, he would have been absolutely certain that Yeshua wouldn't leave him and that he had nothing to be afraid of. Unfortunately, everything happened contrary to his expectations. Yeshua didn't come. The days of sickness became days filled not only with physical suffering, but also days filled with the incredible sorrow of being forsaken and not understanding why the Lord had not come, and why His attitude towards him had changed. The pain of being abandoned by God would have been more bitter and unbearable than his physical torment, and I do not exclude the possibility that it was because of this that Lazarus finally stopped fighting. The life which he considered bereft of Yeshua's love was completely meaningless to him. He simply stopped holding onto it, relaxing his grip and falling back into the depths of death. Lazarus died despite all his own hopes and expectancies, and despite the faith of his sisters who expected Yeshua up until the last minute. He was laid in the tomb and shut up with the stone. Now, with Yeshua standing before the tomb these two realities, the inner and outer, the invisible and visible, God's and man's, arrive at a seemingly insurmountable contradiction with each other. In God's invisible, spiritual reality Lazarus is chosen and beloved, but here in the visible, physical,

---

[277] John 11:38

human reality he is abandoned and rejected by the Lord, and on top of everything else, he is dead.

Get ready. Together with Yeshua we are now coming to the most exciting part of our story, where God's reality becomes fully visible or conversely, where the physical, visible reality is transformed at His touch and for the first time begins to coincide with God's reality. Note that on the path to this transformation from visible reality into that of God's, the first step is left up to us. *'Take away the stone,'* Yeshua tells the sisters; Martha, perplexed and embarrassed, answers, *'Lord, by this time there is a stench, for he has been dead four days.'*[278] Really, she means to say, what for? Why does He require this of them? Does He intend to add the horrifying shame of the *stench* onto the grief of losing a brother and the bitterness of abandonment? How often are we ashamed and unwilling, how unpleasant it is, to let the Lord into the places of *stench,* but *faith is... the evidence of things not seen,* and it is to this faith that Yeshua is calling the sisters. *'Did I not say to you that if you would believe you would see the glory of God?'*[279] His spiritual law is such that until we overcome our own selves and remove the stone, the miracle of resurrection cannot take place. Only when the sisters, having believed, in faith *took away the stone from the place where the dead man was,*[280] and the smell of decay emanating from there, more convincing than any words, confirmed the irreversibility of the facts, and they sensed their own helplessness more intensely than ever before in the face of the incontrovertible, unavoidable physical reality, could He then truly perform the miracle. This is when the Lord *cried with a loud voice, 'Lazarus, come forth!'*[281]

The Lord, *who gives life to the dead and calls those things which do not exist as though they did,*[282] spoke to the one who had been dead, called him by name and brought him back to life. Do you realize that only God has life-giving power? Only God can revive and restore a life; even in those cases when believers do it

---

[278] John 11:39
[279] John 11:40
[280] John 11:41
[281] John 11:43
[282] Rom. 4:17

in His name, there is a huge difference between how people do it and how He does it. Read, for example, the description of how the prophet Elisha raises the child from the dead. He prays, he warms his body, he stretches himself out on him and prays again, and then the Lord answers him and the child comes back to life.[283] The Lord, on the other hand, gives life in exactly the same way he creates: with all the authority of His Word. *Then God said, 'Let there be light'; and there was light.*[284] In every Gospel story where Yeshua raises the dead, He simply **speaks**: *'Talitha, cumi!,'*[285] *'Lazarus, come forth!' 'Young man, I say to you, arise,'*[286] and the life-giving power of His Word raises the dead. It is with this Word that Yeshua brought Lazarus back to life: *and he who had died came out.*[287]

What was it all for?

And so, Lazarus is alive once again. The recent contradiction between God's inner, invisible reality and man's external, visible reality now no longer exists. Lazarus is alive not only in God's spiritual dimension but in the physical, visible dimension as well, and as everyone around now understands, he is beloved and chosen of the Lord. Now that the miracle has taken place and Lazarus has been brought back to life, let's try to answer the principle question of our story: for what, in the end, were Lazarus' sickness and death required? All those days until Yeshua came, the residents of Bethany thought that the Lord had stopped loving him; seeing the tears of Yeshua, many realized that He had not forsaken and rejected Lazarus, but that *He loved him.* When the Lord raised Lazarus from the dead, however, His love and His unique relationship with him became readily visible to all. So, if the Lord did not stop loving him for a second, why then did Lazarus have to suffer and die? *'Could not this*

---

[283] see 2 Kings 4:32-36
[284] Gen. 1:3
[285] Mark 5:41
[286] Luke 7:14
[287] John 11:44

Man, who opened the eyes of the blind, also have kept this man from dying?'[288]

There is a remarkable passage in the *Torah* which the Lord pointed out to me specifically in connection with our central theme of God's restrained love. In Leviticus chapter twenty-one where it speaks about what the priests should and shouldn't do, among other things it says:

> *He who is the high priest among his brethren, on whose head the anointing oil was poured and who is consecrated to wear the garments, shall not uncover his head nor tear his clothes; nor shall he go near any dead body, nor defile himself for his father or his mother...*[289]

Don't you see? The *high priest*, appointed to represent God and display His character, must continue to do his job, withholding his love, restraining his sorrow and compassion, even when the matter concerns people very dear to him. God is revealing Himself on these pages as One who withholds His love and compassion from those who are precious to Him, and with breaking heart and tears held back He continues to carry out His plan. If there is something yet left unsaid in this chapter, then it is the answer to the question of His plan: of what, essentially, does God's plan for Israel consist? What is He showing us here through His plan for Lazarus? For whose sake did Lazarus fall ill and die? For whose sake is everything happening to Israel that is happening?

I don't know if you have noticed that in asking the question regarding the meaning of Lazarus' suffering, we have subsequently formed two completely different questions, which at first glance appear to be almost identical: **Why** did Lazarus have to die? And, **for what purpose** were his sickness and death required? I learned through the story of Job that very frequently with human suffering there is no answer to the question "what did he do to deserve this?" Similarly, there is no answer to the question "why?" in the case of Lazarus. At that time, the Lord

---

[288] John 11:37
[289] Lev. 21:10-11

revealed to me that the true question of all suffering is not "for what sin?" but "for what purpose?" In John chapter eleven the answer to this question is made up of several verses. First of all, before going back to Judea, Yeshua tells his disciples, *'And I am glad for your sakes that I was not there, that you may believe.'*[290] **I was not there, that you may believe!** We still do not have the slightest idea what the Lord is planning to do, but it is already becoming clear that in some mysterious way Yeshua's absence, his distance from the suffering Lazarus, will become someone else's opportunity to believe!

This train of thought continues when the Lord prays at Lazarus' tomb, right before He raises him from the dead, and we find out that everything is happening for *'the people who are standing by... that they may believe that You sent Me.'*[291] Among *the people*, clustered around Lazarus' tomb that day, there were probably many who not so long ago had explained to Lazarus' sisters that his sickness and death was the consequence of his sins and problems. But now the Lord, the only One who knew that this sickness was *for the glory of God*, has come and it turns out that everything that happened to Lazarus had in fact been His plan, designed primarily for their benefit, *that they may believe.*

I have no doubts that sickness and suffering, as well as death and resurrection, changed Lazarus too and that he came forth from the grave renewed not only physically; however, nothing is said about this in the entire chapter. The Author consistently emphasizes the one circumstance that by all accounts was very important to Him. This story was necessary in order that *many believe. Then many of the Jews who had come to Mary, and had seen the things Jesus did, believed in Him.*[292] Even turning the page to the next chapter we find mention that *a great many of the Jews knew that He was there; and they came, not for Jesus' sake only, but that they might also see Lazarus, whom He had raised from the dead.*[293] Once again, I have no doubts that Lazarus emerged from the grave a

---

[290] John 11:15
[291] John 11:42
[292] John 11:45
[293] John 12:9

new man and that this whole story bore its fruit in his own heart as well, yet the target audience of all his suffering and expectancy, his death and resurrection, was *the people,* those who witnessed this miracle or heard about it later. Job mainly suffered "for the purpose of" his own heart being reborn; Lazarus' suffering was allowed by the Lord "for the purpose of" changing and transforming the hearts of others.

For the sake of many

Here I again must return to Israel, for it is not by accident that the Lord placed these two accounts before my mind's eye into a spiritually unified whole. Just as in the story of Lazarus, all that has been happening to Israel has been primarily for others, for *the people,* in order that the nations of the world, formerly separated from the riches of God, could become partakers of these riches. *For God has committed them all to disobedience, that He might have mercy on all.*[294] God has committed, has consecrated, has bound Israel over to a special purpose. From the very moment when the Gospel began to reach the Gentiles, the Heavenly Father led Israel aside, to the altar, into captivity, into a cave or a tomb if you will, just as Abraham led his son up the mountain. As we said in the Prologue, this is not treachery or deception, but the mystery and secret of sonship, of God's election purposes... the mystery of God's love. The Lord has committed His beloved son, His firstborn, over to a prison-like cave of death in order to bring life to those who *were dead in [their] trespasses and the uncircumcision of [their] flesh.*[295] **Israel was bound over to death, as Isaac was bound to the altar, so that the Gentiles could receive life.** This is what Paul means when speaking about the Israelites in his Epistle to the Romans; he declares that the Gentiles *have now* **obtained mercy through their** *[Israel's]* **disobedience.**[296]

---

[294] Rom. 11:32
[295] Col. 2:13
[296] Rom. 11:30

I address you today as true believers in Jesus, as those who know the riches of His glory, and to whom God has already called *out of darkness into His marvelous light.*[297] Remember the suffering of those who were led away from the light into darkness and who were committed over to death. Remember that they were bound over into this darkness and death so that you could walk in the light, so that you could live. That same mystery of God's love which the human mind cannot conceive, the love restrained for the sake of God's plan that we find in the story of Lazarus, is revealed to us in the striking words of Paul: *concerning the gospel, they are* **enemies for your sake,** *but concerning the election they are* **beloved for the sake of the fathers.**[298] Yeshua loved Lazarus, His heart was breaking under the weight of pain and compassion, but for the sake of *many,* for the sake of *the people,* He led him down a path of suffering and death. This same Lord is restraining His love for Israel, holding back the tears of pain and compassion. He has made His *beloved* to be His *enemies,* and has *committed* them to suffering and death for the sake of many, for the sake of the peoples, *for your sake.*

Why did God's plan for Israel have to be this way? What could possibly force the Almighty God to *give the dearly beloved of [His] soul into the hand of her enemies?*[299] Could not the omnipotent Creator of the Universe establish His will and carry out His plan in some way other than condemning His people to suffering? Such a question is similar to a related one often asked by non-believers: wasn't there another way than the bloody sacrifice of Golgotha? Why did Yeshua have to die? Couldn't the Almighty accomplish His plan without the death of His Son? Why did Yeshua have to suffer, and why must Israel suffer?

We can attempt to answer this question only very approximately, because there is no task more hopeless than trying to translate the plans and feelings of God into the language of human questions and answers. In war, for instance, there are situations when the assignment on which a commander

---

[297] 1 Pet. 2:9
[298] Rom. 11:28
[299] Jer. 12:7

146

must send his troops is incredibly dangerous and difficult, nearly impossible. He is forbidden from going himself, so out of moral considerations he can send only someone especially dear to him. His heart goes with him and this is practically the same thing as going himself. In effect, this is what happens with the Lord. Without sacrifice and blood, the salvation God provides is simply not possible, but for the blood sacrifice He can send only the one who is infinitely precious, the one whom He has called His son. This is true in the case of Yeshua, and it is true in the case of Israel. Although our minds cannot accommodate the enormity of God's sacrifice, cannot take in the full horror of this scene, it is vital to the Lord that those who love Him at least know about His pain, His suffering, about His love withheld at the altar. It is important to Him that we know that He, *groaning in Himself,* weeps in the inner room, and that He weeps despite the fact that the hour of resurrection is approaching.

Take away the stone

I want to conclude this chapter with a brief story. A few days ago we took our son to the Western Wall for the first time. He had been eagerly expecting this visit for a long time and was very excited the whole way there. While we passed through the walls of the Old City he constantly asked us, pointing to the walls: is it this one? Is this the *Kotel?* When we had finally completed all the security checks and had squeezed our way through the security officers' narrow booth, we at last found ourselves on the square before the Western Wall. But instead of the rapture and excitement we expected to hear, I heard a small sigh of disappointment: "What? That's the *Kotel?* That tiny little thing?"

I cannot convey what these words did to me and what I experienced at that moment. My husband took my son over to the men's side of the Wall, but I did not stir from where I was. Standing before the "tiny little" *Kotel,* I had the distinct sensation of being lifted up into the air, as it were, and seeing everything from above. I could see the square, this impasse of a wall and the mass of people, both men and women, cordoned off from the Temple Mount and from everything most holy that this Mountain embodies (including the sacrifice of Isaac). Blockaded in by the stony Wall, they seemed to be struggling, pounding against this dead-end barrier and finding no way of escape, no way to break through and reach freedom... Slowly, as if in a dream, I went up to the Wall and felt the stone. I understood at that moment that I was seeing with my physical eyes the spiritual reality that the Lord has been revealing in this chapter. God Himself has *committed* Israel over to suffering, He Himself closed the opening with a stone similar to how the stone was laid over the opening to the tomb of Lazarus – *it was a cave, and a stone lay against it*[300] – and all that was left for us, all we could do, was to beat against these stones, praying and believing that the One who closed us in with the stone yet hears our prayers...

I want to be extremely cautious in saying all this. There are many people considering themselves Christians who will read these lines with great joy. "Yes," they will say, "we also know that Israel is in a situation with no way out; they are suffering and beating themselves against the dead stones of the 'Wailing Wall', whereas Jesus has led us to life and freedom..." Do not confuse me with such as these! Again I repeat, it is not punishment, just as the sickness of Lazarus was not punishment. Such is the nature of our election; it is full of pain, sacrifice, loneliness and tears. At the same time, these tears are not only ours – they are His tears, as well. They are the tears of His love and compassion He is faithfully revealing in this book.

Happily, as in the story of Lazarus, *this sickness is not unto death, but for the glory of God. 'Take away the stone,'* says the Lord, and that dead stone, which it would seem was good only for hiding, entombing and barricading, suddenly becomes the beginning, the way out, the birth canal from which new life springs. *'Remove the stone'* is said to those who, similar to the sisters of Lazarus, live on prayer, hope and expectancy of His coming for the one whom He loves. *Prepare the way for the people!*[301] Our election is

---

300 John 11:38
301 Is. 62:10

that of Lazarus, and as in the story of Lazarus, the stone will be moved away and *living waters shall flow from Jerusalem.*[302] Great joy and a great miracle await the one whom He took by the hand and led into sickness and suffering. *'Then you shall know that I am the LORD, when I have opened your graves, O my people, and brought you up from your graves.'*[303]

Without this resurrection the plan of God is not yet complete, and until it is completed it will remain invisible. At the moment when it all appears to be over, the most wonderful and exciting part in all our stories begins, the part in which *the evidence of things not seen* becomes tangible and the *substance of things hoped for* a rewarding reality. The invisible becomes visible. Yeshua comes to Lazarus in order to justify, heal and raise up. He comes in order to break open the prison of gloom and death where Lazarus was placed for the sake of others in accordance with His plan. He comes in order to say, "Lazarus, come forth!" In this same way, when the predetermined time comes, *rejoice with Jerusalem, and be glad with her, all you who love her; rejoice for joy with her, all you who mourn for her,*[304] because the Lord, no longer able to restrain Himself (ולא-יכל להתאפק) will come to Israel. He will come in order to justify the one who has been slandered for so long. *And all those who despised you shall fall prostrate at the soles of your feet.*[305] He will come in order to break open the prison of gloom and death, to free Israel from their incarceration, to lead them out of the darkness and suffering into which they were imprisoned in accordance with His plan. He will *say to the prisoners, 'Go forth,' to those who are in darkness, 'Show yourselves.'*[306] He comes to raise up and give life. *After two days He will revive us; on the third day He will raise us up, that we may live in His sight.*[307] The Lord, who weeps over the suffering of Jerusalem, will come to her in order to make visible the invisible, to pour out the love so long restrained on the one who was considered rejected and abandoned, and to forever remain with

---

[302] Zech. 14:8
[303] Ezek. 37:13
[304] Is. 66:10
[305] Is. 60:14
[306] Is. 49:9
[307] Hos. 6:2

His beloved. *And the name of the city from that day shall be: THE LORD IS THERE.*[308]

[308] Ezek. 48:35

CHAPTER FOUR

*God will provide for Himself the lamb
for a burnt offering.* (Gen. 22:8)

*Yet we esteemed Him stricken, smitten
by God and afflicted. But He was wounded
for our transgressions, He was bruised
for our iniquities.* (Is. 53:4-5)

*Worthy is the Lamb who was slain to receive power and riches and
wisdom, and strength and honor and glory and blessing!*[309] What
believer in Yeshua has not at least once sung these words from
the Book of Revelation, used repeatedly as they are in the songs
of adoration that can be heard rising up from our gatherings?
The Lamb has been one of the central symbolic images of the
Christian religion since the very first centuries of its existence.
Are you aware, however, that apart from Revelation there is
only one other passage in the entire New Testament where
Yeshua is referred to directly as the Lamb? This occurs in the
first chapter of the Gospel of John where John the Baptist,
inspired by the Holy Spirit, utters this enigmatic exclamation:
'Behold! The Lamb of God who takes away the sin of the world!' A bit
further on, he repeats his announcement: *'Behold the Lamb of
God!'*[310] We find this title in only one chapter outside of
Revelation and repeated in no other place! The realization that

---

[309] Rev. 5:12
[310] John 1:29,36

the Lamb is not mentioned in the other Gospels and is all but absent from the other books of the New Testament as well evokes countless questions, at least for me. Where does John take this image from? What did John the Baptist mean by these words? What meaning did the Israelite observers assign to his words, and finally, why do no other Gospel writers call Yeshua the Lamb?

There is only one reliable source to which we can turn in our search for answers to all these questions: the *Tenach*, naturally. Let's spend some time listening to God's conversation with Israel about the Lamb, to His barely audible whisper wafting up from the well of our history, from the depths of His dealings with us. The Lord never speaks without purpose. Initially, this image is reserved a place among the mysteries of God by only a faint spiritual underscoring, but it is nevertheless clear that the time would eventually arrive for its fulfillment, its incarnation, for it to finally take on flesh and blood, becoming endued with meaning and content. The lines that originally identify this image pulsate with a deep, spiritual significance; they obscure the hidden meanings that must be illuminated to our hearts before we can fully comprehend the way this image is subsequently manifested through God's plan.

The *Akedah* lamb

I think it will surprise you to discover that the Hebrew word for lamb (שה) appears in the Tenach not so many times, and most of the appearances of this word lamb in the Bible bear a distinctly direct relationship to our current discussion. It is not difficult to guess where we first meet the word lamb in the *Tenach* – naturally, this happens in the *Akedah*! When Isaac is being led to the mountain by his father, he asks Abraham, *'Look, the fire and the wood, but where is the lamb for a burnt offering?'*[311] As with each component of the *Akedah* story, this conversation between Abraham and Isaac is, of course, far from idle chat; it is of vital

---

[311] Gen. 22:7

importance both to the destiny of our people and to the fate of all mankind as a whole. Stop for a moment and listen: notes crucial to our melody are being formed at this juncture in time. A word is being pronounced, a question asked. While it has yet to unfold as a separate theme in the spiritual story of Israel, the introductory chord is beginning to sound… cautiously, timidly, not yet knowing its own strength or depth. The Lamb looking *as though it had been slain*[312] from the Book of Revelation starts here with Isaac's innocent, trusting, almost naïve question, *'Where is the lamb for a burnt offering?'* Abraham's answer is astounding in its depth and prophetic meaning: *'My son, God will provide for Himself the lamb for a burnt offering.'*[313] Looking from our day and age back on the hill of Golgotha silhouetted on the horizon next to Mount Moriah, we can make out two identical peaks, two Mounts, clearly visible against the backdrop of heavens darkened from horror. On one a father who is destined to become the father of a nation wields a knife over his only son, through whom his countless descendants are promised; on the other a Son, with the full permission of His Father and under His direction, is crucified on a cross for the salvation of all mankind. Looking back, we can say that the Lord truly did provide Himself a Lamb, and in this sense the prophetic words and the prophetic scene of Mount Moriah finally received their fulfillment.

This is what is traditionally extracted from this story, the meaningful layer which God has already unsealed and revealed to us all, but today I want to humbly ask Him to help us penetrate deeper, to see what is not yet revealed, to view something that until the most recent of times was one of the *secret things [that] belong to the LORD our God.*[314] Let's probe further into Abraham's answer in the original text. In Hebrew (אלוהים יראה-לו השה לעלה בני), these words sound even more profound, even more ambiguous, lending themselves to multiple interpretations. A traditional reading will place a comma in this sentence before the last word בני *(my son)*, such as in the NIV, for

---

[312] Rev. 5:6
[313] Gen. 22:8
[314] Deut 29:29

instance: *'God himself will provide the lamb for the burnt offering, my son.'* Some versions, such as the NKJV we are using here, even move these words to the beginning of the sentence: *'My son, God will provide for Himself the lamb for a burnt offering.'* In the original Hebrew text of the *Tenach*, however, there were no punctuation marks and therefore it is perfectly allowable to divide this sentence in a way other than how the English translations render it. When doing so, a completely different text emerges:

אלוהים יראה-לו... השה לעלה בני

The Lord will provide

In English this would sound approximately as follows: God will provide (for Himself); the lamb for the burnt offering is my son. Naturally, our ears are much better tuned to the translation of Abraham's answer we find in our English Bibles, and therefore the traditional reading tends to appear a more valid rendition. Yet in the original sentence, again, there is nothing substantial that would incline us to support one reading above the other. Who can conclusively defend the position that the Holy Spirit put into the mouth of Abraham the variation of the answer we have become accustomed to in the English translation and that He never intended the other? It would seem to me, for example, that the fact that Abraham named the place The-LORD-Will-Provide – is in itself a satisfactorily weighty – [315]יהוה יראה argument in favor of the alternative reading, supporting the case that God saw this sentence as consisting of dual parts, of two very important statements: אלוהים יראה-לו (God will provide for Himself) and השה לעלה בני (the lamb for the burnt offering is my son). Let us note that, in addition, two meanings can be read into our new text. In one sense, we can assume that the second part refers exclusively to Abraham, who is letting Isaac know what role is prepared for him in the burnt offering: God will provide (for Himself); but for this burnt offering, says Abraham, you my son will be the lamb.

---

[315] Gen. 22:14

It seems to me that we need to dig even deeper, though. Not just intellectually, but with all my inner being I sense that in the words השה לעלה בני we are brushing the surface of one of God's great mysteries. The secret captured inside these words is nestled within the general text as if sealed and sheltered by it. As we begin to break its seal, as we open it up and bring it out into the light, this secret resembles a frail bird that sits trembling on your opened hand which, in order to release to its freedom, you first had to pluck from its cage and grip tightly in both hands. It is alive, it quivers, you want to touch it and at the same time you are afraid to startle it. Let us reach out and caress these words. Let us gently handle this mystery together. The great revelation of God's sonship as never before understood is trembling on your opened palm. So much in the history and destiny of Israel will come into focus if you can but hear what God the Father is speaking through Abraham's words: *the lamb for the burnt offering is My son.* Can you hear the whisper of His voice? The one whom God has called His son is destined to become the lamb. השה לעלה בני – **The lamb for the burnt offering is My son.** With such a reading, the story of the *Akedah* is revealed as but an illustration of God's invisible mystery concealed within the words of Abraham. It also is the perfect illustration for this book, which was given to me by the Lord specifically in order to touch upon this great mystery and not to be afraid of unsealing it: to reach out and explore the depths of God's love, to uncover His mystery of sonship. God will provide Himself a lamb for the burnt offering. God will provide Himself a lamb in His son. השה לעלה בני

❊ ❊ ❊

The *Pesach* lamb

The next time we meet up with a lamb, this of course is in the Book of *Shemot*,[316] in chapter twelve which details the story of the Exodus from Egypt. Again, this story is deeply connected to

---

[316] The Hebrew name for Exodus

our discussion: like the *Akedah*, *Pesach*[317] holds a unique place in God's plan for Israel as well as His plan for Yeshua. Reading this chapter from the very beginning, we again find a lamb. God instructed that the lamb to be slain the eve of the Exodus be separated out four days beforehand.

> *On the tenth of this month every man shall take for himself a lamb... Your lamb shall be without blemish, a male of the first year... Now you shall keep it until the fourteenth day of the same month. Then the whole assembly of the congregation of Israel shall kill it at twilight. And they shall take some of the blood and put it on the two doorposts and on the lintel of the houses where they eat it.*[318]

Doubtless, this passage is one of the most central in the *Tenach* for all who believe in God's Word, for it is here that we first find the image of the sacrificial lamb as a basis for salvation. The slain lamb, with whose blood the doorposts were stained, was a symbol or promise, the basis for Israel's salvation from Egypt. The Lamb looking *as though it had been slain,*[319] with whose blood the heart of the one who accepts His sacrifice is anointed, is the symbol, promise, and basis for the salvation Yeshua brought to the earth. If we reread the first verses of Exodus chapter twelve and compare them with the narratives describing Yeshua's last days and hours on that *Pesach,* we can see that everything that happened to Yeshua (who, as John the Baptist said, was sent to Israel as the *Lamb of God),* including the exclamation, *'His blood be on us and on our children,'*[320] was the full, literal manifestation of the same scenario God gave us in the Book of Exodus. Everything that happened with the Lamb of God, slain during the time of *Pesach* two thousand years ago, precisely fulfilled the role God assigned to the sacrificial lamb during the time of the Exodus.

---

317 Passover
318 Ex. 12:3-7
319 Rev. 5:6
320 Mat. 27:25

A lamb without spot

Several years ago the Lord gave me a script for a children's *Pesach* play. I had never been much interested in the theater and had neither before nor since written a play, but this one seemed to just appear out of the blue, sent directly from heaven itself. I myself was so shaken by what the Lord showed me that I not only wrote the play but set it on the children from our congregation as well. The events the play describes take place in Egypt right before the Exodus. The main character is a Hebrew boy called Avi who has a favorite pet lamb (a male one, of course), which is his constant companion and favorite play-mate. When the Lord gives the order through Moses to separate out a lamb for the sacrifice, Avi's family settles their choice on that lamb, possibly because he was the very best, or perhaps because he was just the only one there was. The evening before the Exodus, Avi's parents go to catch the lamb to slay it, and the crying boy chases after them, all the time asking, "Why? Why him? He is so good, so white, so clean and pure!" His parents answer, "This is the reason we are choosing him; because he is spotless, he is the one that must be used for the sacrifice. Later you'll understand why we could not act otherwise and the reason that he needs to die." That night when, ready to leave Egypt, all the family members including the tearful boy sit at the table sharing the first ever Passover *seder* in the history of Israel, suddenly there is complete silence. Then, first from one, then from another house we hear horrified shrieks and wails. The boy, utterly frightened, is held close by his parents and when he looks up into their faces, inquisitively waiting for an explanation, his mother explains, "Now do you understand why your lamb had to die? On this night the angel of death is striking all the firstborn sons of Egypt. You are our firstborn, and if not for the blood of the lamb on our doorposts, you would have died too. With his death he gave you life." With tears in his eyes, the shaken Avi gives thanks to God for His provision of salvation.

I have related this scene to help us understand how everything that happened to Yeshua exactly fulfilled the scenario laid out by God during the time of the Exodus. According to the synoptic Gospels, Yeshua was arrested on Thursday, the fourteenth day of the month, on the eve of Passover; four days before this, on Sunday, the tenth day of the month, He entered Jerusalem and began preparations for His sacrifice. At one point in the play the boy's parents seem cruel and inhumane in the eyes of their son, but they were simply following God's instructions, saving his life by means of the blood of the sacrificial lamb. The crucifixion of Yeshua was also cruel and inhumane, but through it God's plan for salvation was accomplished through the shed blood of the sacrificial Lamb.

The silent sufferer

So, **God will provide Himself a lamb in His son** – this is the theme that flows through the *Akedah*. **The sacrificial lamb as a basis for salvation** is the image given in Exodus. The third time we find a significant mention of a lamb in the *Tenach* is as fundamental in relation to Israel, as in relation to Yeshua. This is the famous fifty-third chapter of Isaiah, which long ago became a stone of stumbling between Christians and Jewish people: the former read it as a prophecy of the atoning death of the Messiah, while the latter assert that Isaiah is prophetically describing the suffering of the people of Israel. In the seventh verse of this chapter we read: *He was led as a lamb to the slaughter, and as a sheep before its shearers is silent, so He opened not His mouth.* In this song of the Greatly Suffering One, we begin to hear a third motif, without which the Biblical image of the lamb is incomplete: humbly and silently, the lamb carries the sufferings laid on him for the sake of others. **The substitutionary suffering of the meek and humble lamb** is the third motif connected with this image that we find in the *Tenach*.

In a new, deeper and more meaningful way, the Spirit of God is now illuminating for us the meaning of the words He placed in the mouth of John the Baptist in the beginning of John's Gospel. In the words, *'Behold! The Lamb of God who takes away the sin of the world,'* all three of God's mysteries which we have examined are fused into a united whole. The *Lamb of God* means that this is the Son of God (השה לעלה בני – Gen. 22) and that His substitutionary suffering (Is. 53) will become the basis for salvation (Ex. 12). It is probable that the historian of culture or religion studying "the rise of Christianity" will remain in the dark as to how the images from all these rather unconnected motifs merge and unite into a single figure. A believer can be distinguished from a worldly scientist, however, in that he understands *not in words taught... by human wisdom but in words taught by the Spirit, expressing spiritual truths in spiritual words.*[321] Things that cannot be associated in man's wisdom are somehow associated in His. All that the Lord spoke to Israel during their history has found fulfillment in the substitutionary suffering of God's Son.

Riches for the Gentiles

So now that the words about Yeshua's substitutionary suffering have been pronounced, let us turn to Romans chapter eleven. In reference to Israel, Paul writes, *'Now if their fall is riches for the world, and their failure riches for the Gentiles, how much more their fullness... for if their being cast away is the reconciling of the world, what will their acceptance be but life from the dead?'*[322] Usually those who analyze these verses are interested in the positive, forward-looking aspect of these spiritual syllogisms: fullness, acceptance, life from the dead. For me, in contrast, the statements Paul places in the first, conditional portions are also crucial: *their being cast away is reconciling of the world; their fall is riches for the world; their failure [is] riches for the Gentiles.* I do not doubt that you have read these words before, but do you realize the full import of their meaning? The thought contained in the second part of verse twelve, *their failure [is] riches for the Gentiles,* can be rephrased and expressed in the following manner: Israel has failed so that the Gentiles could become rich through their failure. Put in such a way it is easy to see that these words are perfectly symmetrical to what was said about Yeshua in the second Epistle to the Corinthians: *though He was rich, yet for your sakes He became poor,*

---

[321] 1 Cor. 2:13 (NIV)
[322] Rom. 11:12,15

that you through His poverty might become rich.[323] Does not the parallel surprise you? We have *become rich* through the *poverty* of Yeshua; the Gentiles have obtained *riches* due to the *failure* of Israel.

Moreover, down in the fifteenth verse, when Paul says that through the casting away of Israel the world is reconciled with God, the same association comes up. Whom do we usually think about when we speak of reconciliation? Yeshua, of course. There is no doubt that Paul, perhaps even more than anyone else, clearly saw Yeshua's redeeming sacrifice as the basis, the payment for the reconciliation of the world to God. Note however, that this does not at all prevent him from also believing that this reconciliation could happen only in conjunction with the casting away of Israel and he does not see any sort of contradiction in this. For Paul, in some mysterious, incomprehensible way – *Oh the depth of the riches both of the wisdom and knowledge of God! How unsearchable are His judgments and His ways past finding out!*[324] – the casting away of Israel, that is, Israel's rejection of Yeshua and all the ensuing suffering of our people, carries a redemptive significance, a substitutionary function, which in this sense makes it similar to the way Yeshua's suffering had redemption as its purpose.

A great mystery

Although at first I did not intend to broach the subject of Paul's writings in this book, I sense the Spirit urging me to comment on these lines from Romans. Rooted in the authority of all possible churches and confessions, the two-thousand-year-old tradition of the Christian reading of Paul so "domesticated" and distorted his teaching beyond recognition that it turned him into the father and author of sanctioned anti-Semitism. It is possible that this is the reason I am compelled to devote at least a few lines to this believer in Yeshua, this *Pharisee, the son of a Pharisee,*[325] who

---

[323] 2 Cor. 8:9
[324] Rom. 11:33
[325] Acts 23:6

served God *as [his] forefathers did.*[326] Obviously, Paul does in fact write about the *failure* of Israel, about their *fall* and *their casting away;* he writes that they *were blinded,*[327] and says they have become *enemies for your sake.*[328] Does not all this mean that this Jewish scholar who became the Apostle to the Gentiles in fact sincerely believed his people to be rejected by God?

Let's try to sort this out together. In the epistle to the Romans, Paul reveals to believers a mystery, a secret he hopes will help them understand God's plan and not look down upon Israel. *'For I do not desire, brethren, that you should be ignorant of this mystery...'*[329] What is the mystery intended to prevent the high-mindedness of the Gentiles? The difficulty in answering this question becomes evident when we begin to examine the usual interpretations, attempting to explain the mystery Paul is revealing as being contained in his famous phrase: *and so all Israel will be saved.*[330] What exactly is the mystery? If *all Israel* is understood as being Jewish people who believe in Yeshua, the Roman Christians should never have been in doubt of their salvation. If *Israel* is to be understood as the Church, made up of Jewish and Gentile believers, again, this salvation should not be a secret for anyone. If, finally, it means that all of the people of Israel will be saved after the mission of the Gentiles is complete and the full number of Gentiles comes in, then first of all, it is unclear in what way such a sequence – first the Gentiles and then the Jewish people – should ward off the Gentile-Christians' arrogance. Secondly, the salvation and restoration of all Israel is promised repeatedly in the Scriptures and is not really a mystery by any means. So what exactly is the mystery that Paul wanted to reveal to the Romans?

It seems to me that the mystery Paul is referring to is not found in the fact that the once stumbling and hardened Israel will eventually be saved, although it is completely possible that it was necessary to remind the Roman Christians about this. I

---

[326] 2 Tim. 1:3
[327] Rom. 11:7
[328] Rom. 11:28
[329] Rom. 11:25
[330] Rom. 11:26

believe that the mystery the Apostle was given to reveal is formulated in the next verse down: verse twenty-eight, which we have repeatedly quoted on these pages. This verse, a key one for our book, is made up of two affirmations: *concerning the gospel they are **enemies for your sake,** but concerning the election they are **beloved for the sake of the fathers.*** What does Paul want to tell us with these words?

Two realities

Let's return for a minute to the story of Benjamin and the two lines – visible and invisible – which we spoke about in the second chapter. At that dramatic moment when the cup is extracted from the sack and the stares of the men – whether perplexed or condemning, hateful or compassionate – are fixed on their younger brother, we can easily discern these two lines, these two realities that not only don't seem to match up but actually oppose and contradict each other. In the visible one, Benjamin is hated and despised. He appears to be the thief and **enemy** and neither he nor his brothers can even imagine what the other line might be. At that moment the reality of **the inner room** is invisible, completely hidden from the view of the brothers. In the true, invisible reality Benjamin is *beloved;* Joseph, the author of this whole story and the one in whose name Benjamin is being accused, actually loves his brother infinitely. If we ask why the visible reality contrasts so strikingly with the invisible reality, and why on the visible line Benjamin is made out to be the thief and enemy, then the answer is very simple: for the sake of the brothers. Joseph has enacted this plan so that his brothers could repent. For their sake, for the sake of their change and their transformation, he makes his **beloved** brother into the **enemy** in this plan. Yes, Benjamin carries on himself all the pain and weight of this trial, but the real trial is not for Benjamin but for his brothers. The hearts of the brothers are being tested on Benjamin specifically because he is so dear to Joseph.

After such an expressive illustration, we can better appreciate the secret, the mystery that Paul revealed to the Romans. The Apostle to the Gentiles was trying to convey to his Roman audience the mystery of God's plan for Israel. He wanted them to understand that God's invisible plan differs greatly from the visible circumstances and that besides the visible reality, there exists another, invisible reality, the only true reality. *Faith is the... evidence of things not seen,*[331] and just as in the story with Benjamin, in this invisible reality everything is reversed. Above all else, it was important for the Gentiles to understand that even when Israel seems to be forsaken by God on the level of visible circumstances, in the true, invisible reality the Lord infinitely loves Israel. They are forever the *beloved of the Lord.* This is the first part of the mystery that Paul *does not desire* that they (and we) should be *ignorant* about.

The grafting process

Just as in the story of Benjamin, we might ask ourselves, why is Israel made out to be the enemy in the visible reality? Why are they seen as rejecting and rejected? The next step in our exploration of this mystery asks, **for what purpose** has Israel stumbled, **for what purpose** have they become the enemy? Here Paul reveals the mystery of God's plan for the salvation of the Gentiles, **based upon** the hardening and stumbling of Israel. If we reread the famous lines about the cultivated and wild olive trees that directly precede this discussion about the mystery, where the Gentiles are cautioned against being *wise in [their] own opinion,*[332] it appears that Paul hopes this visual aid will shed some light on this mystery for the Gentiles, thereby helping them avoid high-mindedness and arrogance on the account of their new status. *And if some of the branches were broken off, and you, being a wild olive tree, were grafted in among them, and with them became a partaker of the root and fatness of the olive tree, do not boast against the branches... you do not support the root, but the root*

---

[331] Heb. 11:1
[332] Rom. 11:25

supports you.[333] The Gentile Christians should not think that Israel's stumbling left no room for them and that they are no longer the chosen and beloved people: it's not the branches grafted in that support the root, but the root that supports the branches.

In my lectures on Paul, many times I have drawn on the board this illustration of the olive tree, scene by scene. First I draw the trunk and lots of branches of one color on the trunk. Then some of these branches of that color are left on the tree while the others are made to lie down on the ground next to the tree, after which branches of another color, the wild ones, appear in the vacant places. The branches which are broken off did not just fall off; they were *broken off* **so that** others could be *grafted in,* so that room could be freed up for the branches to be grafted in. In this way, not only the "yes" of the believing root which supports the whole tree, but also the "no" of those broken off, the natural branches of Israel, creates the necessary conditions for the branches of the wild olive tree to be grafted in. It is this sacrifice that made the Gentiles' accession into God's covenant family possible.

In addition, it is not enough for the branches that are grafted in to be simply placed up next to the tree. In order to graft in a branch, you have to make a cut into the tree. Do you understand? It is not enough to simply break off the old, worthless, dried-up branch, but one must cut into the living branch in order to graft the new branch in the vacant place. This cutting, this slicing into the quick of the live tree, is what the Lord did with Israel in order for other nations to be grafted into this tree. The salvation of the Gentiles became possible only at the price of these cuts, these wounds to the living Israel – *enemies for your sake* – and it is this mystery that Paul was trying to get across to the believing Gentiles. In Joseph's plan, his beloved Benjamin was made into the thief, the enemy, for the sake of the brothers. In the plan which the Lord is carrying out, His beloved Israel is made into *enemies* for the sake of the Gentiles, for the sake of the peoples, *for your sake...*

---

[333] Rom. 11:17-18

The path to resurrection

Believers in Yeshua like to explain that when the prophets of Israel foretold the arrival of the Messiah, they could not comprehend the lapse in time between His first and second coming. These prophets saw His arrival as a single event, within which they perceived both His glory and His suffering; they were unable to distinguish between them. Something akin to this is observable in regards to Israel. The prophecies in the *Tenach* speak to us about the glory that awaits the chosen people, and this glory is directly connected to the coming of the Messiah and the subsequent restoration of the Kingdom of Israel. It was not a coincidence that the last question Yeshua's disciples asked Him was specifically concerning this. *'Lord, will You at this time restore the kingdom to Israel?'*[334] Until just the right time none of the disciples could perceive what the Lord knew: that before all the Biblical prophecies could be fulfilled on the way to this glory, Israel would have to endure many centuries of suffering and humiliation for the sake of other peoples. Before the gleaming light of His love could flood over our people, for long millenniums they would be *committed* over to darkness, at times seemingly impenetrable. Yeshua's last words here on the earth must be seen in this context. *'It is not for you to know times or seasons which the Father has put in His own authority.'*[335] In other words, you are to follow the Lord; the Father Himself will take care of the details of fulfilling His promises, accomplishing His plan for His people and restoring the kingdom to Israel.

A profound parallel can be drawn between what He said concerning Israel and what He said concerning Himself when He revealed to the disciples beforehand that He would have to *be killed, and be raised the third day.*[336] During the time before His crucifixion, the disciples were expecting that any day now He would begin His reign, but instead He went through

---

[334] Acts 1:6
[335] Acts 1:7
[336] Mat 16:21

unthinkable suffering and humiliation. He died on the cross and only later rose to eternal glory. Now the disciples, having experienced His resurrection, having recognized and come to believe that He truly is the Lord and Messiah, are still expecting that very soon He will restore the Kingdom of Israel, and that Israel would soon be bathed in the extraordinary glory prophesied in the Scriptures. What is completely hidden from them, however, is that on the path to this glory Israel would first have to pass through long centuries of humiliation and suffering; **they would have to undergo crucifixion before their resurrection.** Without the revelation the Holy Spirit brings, such thoughts are simply incomprehensible, so the Lord did not explain everything to them at that time. This is why God's plan for Israel, their sacrificial election, this laying of Israel on the altar that made salvation available for the nations and everything it entailed, was not revealed to them until Yeshua went to the Father, not until the disciples received the Holy Spirit. The Lord promised, *'When He, the Spirit of truth, has come, He will guide you into all truth.'*[337] This is why He began to reveal this mystery to His chosen witnesses only after His Ascension and the pouring out of the Holy Spirit.

For salvation's sake

We know that in time, Paul also became one of these chosen witnesses. Like Yeshua, Paul unmistakably understood God's two-step plan for His people, a plan in which resurrection is preceded by crucifixion. *Most assuredly, I say to you, unless a grain of wheat falls into the ground and dies, it remains alone; but if it dies, it produces much grain,*[338] and it was Israel's death, necessary in order to produce much fruit, that was revealed to Paul. This is why, when we run up against those frequently confusing passages in his epistles that speak of Israel's *casting away*, we must recognize that Paul did not create the Christian doctrine of replacement, but was prophesying by the Holy Spirit about the

---

[337] John 16:13
[338] John 12:24

things he saw yet to come. The Father was showing him the future. We must understand that with all of his love for Israel, with all his desire to say to his people the words Peter once said to the Lord, *'Far be it from you... this shall not happen to you,'*[339] he simply couldn't write anything else because this was God's plan, this was God's sacrificial choice of Israel. Not only did Paul foresee Israel's casting away and their imminent suffering, the points which scholars like to remind us of in traditional commentaries, but he saw the substitutionary, sacrificial significance of these sufferings – *enemies for your sake* – as well as the Lord's restrained tears as He made Israel the enemy, for the sake of salvation for the nations.

The secret of God's love for Israel, and the mystery of His plan for them that was carried out in order to provide salvation to the nations, was the two-fold mystery of Israel Paul revealed to the Romans. He hoped that in considering the suffering, rejected Yeshua together with the people seemingly rejected by God, the Gentile Christians would not *be haughty,*[340] but would see in this the mystery of God; he wanted them to see in Israel the sacrifice made for the sake of their salvation. Paul exhorts them to keep in mind that the *blindness*[341] of Israel, God's committing them over *to disobedience*[342] and their suffering, was part of His plan and necessary for the Gentiles to *obtain mercy,*[343] to receive salvation. Israel is thus committed over to this disobedience and blindness *until* that time when *the fullness of the Gentiles has come in.*[344] With every possible argument, he strove to communicate to his Roman audience this mystery of God's love. He so desired for the Church to comprehend this secret that she is now only beginning to grasp, that the rejection and suffering of Israel was an indispensable part of God's plan, and that this suffering is of a substitutionary, sacrificial character. He wanted them to know ahead of time that resurrection would be sure to follow crucifixion, and that Israel's suffering, far from voiding their

---

[339] Mat. 16:22
[340] Rom. 11:20
[341] Rom. 11:25
[342] Rom. 11:32
[343] Rom. 11:30
[344] Rom. 11:25

sonship and election in God, on the contrary confirms it. The evidence of this is laid out before you in this book. *Though He was a Son, yet He learned obedience by the things which He suffered.*[345] Yes, in the Book of Romans Paul distinctly saw and wrote about the period of Israel's sacrificial humiliation, belittling and suffering, but together with it he perceived the invisible reality of God's love for Israel, the reality of the inner room, the only place one gets to see what is really on God's heart. This was Paul's desire for the readers of his Epistle to the Romans.

⚜ ⚜ ⚜

We esteemed Him stricken

Let's take a summary glance back at what we have learned. Who did the Lord choose to grace these pages as reflections of Israel? Isaac, led to the altar by his father; Job, beset by all imaginable misfortunes; Benjamin, accused of a crime he did not commit; Lazarus, who ran out of time while waiting for the Lord to rescue him. Tragic characters, tragic images, tragic stories... Perhaps you are already able to distinguish the unifying strain which is heard in one way or another in each chapter of this book. Isaac, Job, Lazarus and Benjamin, with all the diversity of Biblical plots, are united by a single emotion: the horror of bewilderment and incomprehension of what is happening to them and God's love for them, and this is coupled with the fact that the scenarios God designed for each of them were actually the outpouring, the manifestation and expression of this love. Everyone we have spoken of here felt abandoned by God at some moment when in fact, God had never stopped loving them. **The secret of God's love, hidden within His plan** is the theme that is doubtless present in all these stories of people ostensibly "abandoned" by God. At this point, let us turn to the Book of Isaiah, chapter fifty-three.

> *He is despised and rejected by men, a man of sorrows and acquainted with grief. And we hid, as it were, our*

---

[345] Heb. 5:8

faces from Him; He was despised and we did not esteem Him. Surely He has borne our griefs and carried our sorrows; **yet we esteemed Him stricken, smitten by God, and afflicted.**[346]

Many years ago when I read this chapter for the first time, having just become a believer, I was struck by the appalling contrast between the human perception *'yet we esteemed him,'* which sees the one who is afflicted and in pain as being punished by God, and the lofty substitutionary, sacrificial significance of these sorrows, these sufferings borne for the sake of those who scoff, spit and esteem them otherwise. This disparity has been considered at least once by each person through whose heart the story of the Crucifixion has passed. I see the most piercing and tortuous, the most heart-rending lines in the Gospels as the ones in which we witness how Yeshua, willingly undergoing the mocking, suffering and death on the cross, is perceived as being abandoned by God. *And those who passed by blasphemed Him, wagging their heads and saying, 'You who destroy the temple and build it in three days, save Yourself! If You are the Son of God, come down from the cross.'*[347]

Come down from the cross

Believers in Yeshua know that the Lord had to turn His back on the Son of God dying on the cross in order to bring His plan for salvation to completion: 'It is finished!' *For God so loved the world that He gave His only begotten Son, that whoever believes in Him should not perish but have everlasting life.*[348] This is the heavenly mystery that is to *the Jews a stumbling block and to the Greeks foolishness,*[349] the very foundation of our faith. Is it possible to measure and describe the pain of the Father, watching as the Son He sent into the world died the most horrible of all earthly deaths? Yet, He *did not spare His own Son, but delivered Him up for*

---

[346] Is. 53: 3-4
[347] Mat. 27:39-40
[348] John 3:16
[349] 1 Cor. 1:23

us all.[350] We witness here again that same amazing characteristic of God's love that all the stories gathered here testify to: this is how Abraham restrained himself, how Joseph restrained himself, how Yeshua restrained Himself – and how the Father, in sending His Son to the cross, restrained Himself. The Heavenly Father, withholding His tears over Golgotha, reveals to us the love which you and I have already observed over and over in the Bible: love able through tears to lay its beloved on the altar. Could it possibly be otherwise if this is that same God, the God of Abraham, Job, and Joseph? If there is any paradox here, it is only in the sense that the striking resemblance to Israel's situation has remained unnoticed by both Jewish people and Christians alike. The words Yeshua *cried out* on the cross, some of the last words of His earthly life, '*My God, My God, why have You forsaken Me,*'[351] were the words from a Psalm that so perfectly expressed the pain and sorrow, the agonized moan of abandonment, with which the chests of the prophets heaved again and again. Recall the words, *why should You be like… a mighty one who cannot save?*[352]

I pray that the Lord who set me to the task of writing this book would help me say what I now must say, and may He help you hear it, my believing brothers and sisters. Yeshua was considered to be abandoned by God specifically because He was ridiculed and suffering. '*He trusted in God; let Him deliver Him now if He will have Him.*'[353] How ironic that it was later the Christians who did not doubt they were seeing God's punishment and rejection reflected in the suffering and ridicule of Israel during the first centuries! Everything that happened to Yeshua, His humiliation and suffering, down to the very words that mocked Him, were revealed by the Holy Spirit through Israel and through the Scriptures many centuries before His death. Christians, who should have known better than anyone else that being abandoned by God could become (and became!) an element of God's plan, a part of His election and a path to His

---

[350] Rom. 8:32
[351] Mat. 27:46
[352] Jer. 14:9
[353] Mat. 27:43

glory, fell into the same trap in relation to Israel. It was now they who turned out to be the ones that laughingly scorned Israel and their suffering, saying to them, "If you are the son of God, come down from the cross!" Or in other words, if you are still the chosen people, stop your suffering! *"He trusted in God; let Him deliver Him now if He will have Him; for He said, 'I am the Son of God'"*[354] This is what was if not said, then in essence insinuated concerning Israel. Christians saw the mark of God's wrath and rejection in the sufferings of Israel – *yet we esteemed Him stricken, smitten by God, and afflicted* – while these sufferings were endued with a sacrificial meaning. Israel has been offered up as a sacrifice for the sake of other peoples: *enemies for your sake.*

Two sacrifices

In this sense, when the rabbis interpret Isaiah fifty-three as speaking of Israel, they somehow, some way come close to the truth of God, though tracing it through the veil that is still in place. Israel, like Yeshua, is being offered up as a sacrifice for the sake of the peoples, for the sake of the salvation and justification of many. Truly, Israel is being led like a lamb to the slaughter, only to a different sacrifice, a difference slaughter. In the Book of Leviticus we read how on the Day of Atonement there were two offerings: the goat for the sin offering, and the scapegoat to carry the sins on itself.

> *He shall take the two goats and present them before the LORD at the door of the tabernacle of meeting. Then Aaron shall cast lots for the two goats: one lot for the LORD and the other lot for the scapegoat. And Aaron shall bring the goat on which the LORD's lot fell, and offer it as a sin offering... Aaron shall lay both his hands on the head of the live goat, confess over it all the iniquities of the children of Israel, and all their transgressions, concerning all their sins, putting them on the head of the goat, and shall send it away into the*

---

[354] Mat. 27:43

wilderness by the hand of a suitable man. The goat shall bear on itself all their iniquities to an uninhabited land; and he shall release the goat in the wilderness.[355]

Two goats, two sacrifices. One is offered as a sacrifice for sin (meaning that he atones for the sins with his death – this was the type foretelling of Yeshua's atoning death), and the live one carries on itself all the iniquities of the people. Why this way? I do not have an answer to this question, but it was prescribed by God, He established this procedure, and in it I see a very clear shadow and type of the future plan of God. Israel, which in real life so often has truly become the "scapegoat", was chosen by God in order to bear the iniquity of the peoples. God's Son Yeshua was sent in order to die on the cross an atoning death **as a sin offering.** God's son Israel was chosen to be offered as a sacrifice for the sake of other peoples and to be released alive into the wilderness, into the desert, to **bear their iniquity.**

I believe that only by seeing the sonship of the Son of God and the tasks of His election placed side by side with Israel's destiny can we fully comprehend the essence of Israel's sonship and election. I suspect that many people will be unhappy with this analysis of mine. Even Christians who love Israel see punishment for sin and backsliding in everything that has happened to us, and many readers will ask me what sort of parallel can be drawn between the sinless Son of God and the stiff-necked and disobedient Israel. The analogy here is not one of righteousness, and it is clear that any comparison in this sense is not viable. Yeshua had no sin, while in any person, and consequently in any people, sin is found in abundance; Israel does not differ from other nations in this sense. We are speaking here only of election, of calling, of how **the earthly destiny of Israel, just as the earthly destiny of Yeshua, was to be offered as a sacrifice.** Specifically in this lies the essence of God's sonship. There are only two God calls His son, and in the Bible they at times merge into complete indistinguishability. In reading the Psalms we often ask, *'Of whom does the prophet say*

---

[355] Lev. 16:7-9,21-22

this, of himself or of some other man?'[356] Is this passage prophesying about the sufferings of Israel, or about the sufferings of Yeshua? Recall how freely and casually, as something taken for granted, the Gospel of Matthew ascribes to Yeshua prophetic words which were, essentially, spoken concerning Israel: *'Out of Egypt I called My Son.'*[357] There are only two God calls His son in the Bible and about both it may be said that, *though He was a Son, yet He learned obedience by the things which He suffered.*[358]

Up out of the desert

At this point I'd like to make a small digression, a detour in order to see one more totally unexpected and fascinating parallel found in the Word of God. After everything was finished on Mount Moriah, in Genesis chapter twenty-two, verse nineteen it says, *so Abraham returned to his young men, and they rose and went together to Beersheba; and Abraham dwelt at Beersheba.* Does nothing strike you as unusual about this verse? Do you not wonder where Isaac was? Why does it say, *so Abraham returned,* and not a word is said of Isaac? It turns out that after the sacrifice on Mount Moriah was *finished,* Isaac mysteriously disappears from our picture completely. We don't see him again until the very end of chapter twenty-four, which describes his meeting with Rebekah. It says that he came up from the South (i.e. the desert), from the place called *Beer Lahai Roi,*[359] but nothing is said about what had gone on with him all this time in the desert; it is hidden from us. At the very end of chapter twenty-four, however, we witness a fascinating scene. When Rebekah sees Isaac for the first time, coming up out of the desert just then, she literally falls off her camel. The English translation, *she dismounted from her camel,* does not correctly portray the original Hebrew, ותפל מעל הגמל (and she fell off the camel).

---

[356] Acts 8:34

[357] Mat. 2:14, Hosea 11:1

[358] Heb. 5:8

[359] באר לחי ראי, the Well of either the Living One who sees me, or the One who sees me lives.

Why did Rebekah fall? Whether she was staggered by the lingering imprint of the sufferings Isaac had undergone, the indelible stamp of the Mount Moriah experience etched into his expression, or whether he was simply radiating God's glory, we are not told. However, there is no better commentator on the Bible than the Bible itself; therefore, while not knowing for sure exactly what so stunned Rebekah, we can look for an explanation in another part of the Scriptures. We now go to a similar scene. In the Gospel of John, when the soldiers come to the Garden of Gethsemane to arrest Yeshua, He says to them, '*I am He,*' at which point *they drew back and fell to the ground.*[360]

I don't think that any of us would have difficulty in answering the question of why the soldiers fell in the Garden of Gethsemane. The Son of God standing before them, whose weakness, terror and sorrow we had witnessed just a few moments before, was now filled with such authority from God that they simply couldn't stand before Him and thus shaken, they *drew back* and *fell.* Perhaps it was the same with Isaac. The contrite heart, humbling itself before God in the fire of testing, is cleansed and filled with God's glory. Therefore, after the experiences of Mount Moriah and the desert, Isaac must have been resplendent with God's light, dazzling Rebekah as she laid eyes on him for the first time.

For me this story is just one more confirmation of how the Lord, the Author of the Word, unites and combines all these images: the image of Yeshua, the image of Isaac and the image of Israel. Israel also seems to completely disappear from God's plans after the sacrifice of Golgotha was *finished.* This is our time in the desert. *They wandered in the wilderness in a desolate way... hungry and thirsty... [they] sat in darkness and in the shadow of death, bound in affliction and irons...*[361] This is our time of suffering and affliction, which can be survived only by drinking of the living water of *Beer Lahai Roi.* This is our time to be abandoned by all and remain alive only because the One who sees us lives. However, an end to this suffering is coming. The day will arrive

---

360 John 18:6
361 Ps. 107:4-5,10

when Israel will come up out of the wilderness, just as Isaac came up out of the desert shining with God's glory. At that time, the superimposition of the destinies of Israel and Yeshua, today revealed to only a few, will become evident to all. Both are called God's son, both had a supernatural, miraculous birth, both went through their time in the desert. Both ascended the altar and underwent suffering and were apparently abandoned by God in this suffering when in fact both were but accomplishing His plan of salvation. Finally, at the end of their suffering, both are prepared to enter into God's glory.

Two sons

Ultimately, there are two that the Lord calls His son, two whom He chose to suffer for the sake of others. Two were chosen in order to become the sacrificial lamb. **The substitutionary suffering of Israel** is the heading I think I would give to all that the Lord has revealed about Israel in this chapter, or perhaps even in this entire book, whether I would use the material for a presentation at a seminar or a conference. Nevertheless, I am writing a book now, not an academic work, and in my opinion the words the Lord gave me for the book's title portray with surprising accuracy the startling similarity between God's plan for Yeshua and His plan for Israel. Israel, like Yeshua, has been undergoing a substitutionary, sacrificial suffering for the sake of others. Similar to when Yeshua was on the cross, the afflicted Israel has been perceived as forsaken by God. *If You are the Son of God, come down from the cross,*[362] was said two thousand years ago to the One who ascended this cross as the sacrificial Lamb. If we can remember these words that were addressed to the Savior dying on the cross, perhaps we will be able to understand that suffering does not always infer sin and rejection. Then we will be able to answer the question that haunts every Jewish soul, "How could God look at the Holocaust, at the gas chambers, at the agony of torture, at the dying women and children? How can He look today at the exploding buses and mutilated corpses?" (I am

---

[362] Mat. 27:40

completing this book the day after yet another atrocious terrorist attack in Jerusalem.) The answer is the same way He was able to look at Golgotha, the way He watched the suffering and death of Yeshua – *restraining Himself.* He is holding back the pain and tears with self-control. I do not know and will not accept another answer.

In sending His Son to the earth, the God of Israel, the God of Abraham, Isaac and Jacob, offered up two sons as a sacrifice. One is Yeshua, *'This is My beloved Son, in whom I am well pleased,'*[363] who was to **die as a sacrifice for sin;** and the other is Israel, *'Israel is My son, My firstborn,'*[364] who was offered as a **living sacrifice to bear iniquity.** The rejection, suffering and death of God's Son Yeshua were necessary in order for salvation to come into the world. *We were reconciled to God through the death of His Son.*[365] The casting away and suffering of God's son Israel, the rejection, affliction and death of millions of Jewish people, was necessary in order for salvation to reach everyone and for God's plan to be fully accomplished in this world. *Their being cast away is the reconciling of the world.*[366]

The paradox of Abraham's reward

Let's return to our Prologue one final time and look back down at this lonely peak, at the stony mass which overshadows this book from its very first lines. In the *Midrash Raba Bereshit,* from which we have already quoted several times, Abraham says to the Lord, "I could have put up a great protest, when You asked my son of me. But I constrained my pity and brought him as a sacrifice in the fulfillment of Your will. As a reward for this, Lord, I ask that when Isaac's children have hardships that You will remember this *Akedah* and may Your mercy be fulfilled towards them."[367]

---

[363] Mat. 3:17
[364] Ex. 4:22
[365] Rom. 5:10
[366] Rom. 11:15
[367] *Midrash Raba Bereshit,* parashah 56

באים לידי צרה כן יהי רצון מלפניך יי אלהינו בשעה שיהיו בניו יצחק

תזכור להם אותה העקידה ותימלא עליהם רחמים

Doesn't it seem perfectly natural that the one who remained faithful to God through such a serious and frightening trial would have the right to expect blessing for his descendents as a reward? "Remember this *Akedah* and may Your mercy be fulfilled towards them." Indeed, the Lord promises Abraham, *'In your seed all the nations of the earth shall be blessed, because you have obeyed My voice.'*[368] I think Abraham was gratified and that he rejoiced upon hearing these words, being completely convinced that the blessing would be tangible, that it would be of practical benefit to his people and that the Lord had well-being, security, prosperity and honor in mind with which to award the Patriarch's descendants, for his "constraining" his "pity".

The lines of this book come closer to the actual truth, however. While truly giving *exceedingly abundantly above all that we ask or think,*[369] God does not choose our ways but His own to bring us to that which is *exceedingly abundantly above.* This is why Abraham standing on Mount Moriah could not foresee how this story would end, and what this blessing would entail for his people. He did not know that just as he himself, in the words of the Midrash, had "constrained" his "pity" and had brought his own son as a sacrifice, even so the Father, constraining His pity, *restraining* His love and the *yearning* of His *heart* and His *mercies,*[370] would also lead His son Israel to the altar as a sacrifice.

> As a reward and to fulfill His promise, the God of Abraham calls Isaac's descendants His son: *Israel is My son, My firstborn.*[371]

> As a reward and to fulfill His promise, the God of Abraham provides a sacrificial lamb through this

---

[368] Gen. 22:18
[369] Eph. 3:20
[370] Is. 63:15
[371] Ex. 4:22

son: 'the lamb for the burnt offering is my son,'
(השה לעלה בני).[372]

As a reward and to fulfill His promise, the God of Abraham, *restraining* Himself, leads His son through sacrificial suffering by which *all the nations of the earth shall be blessed.*

Life from the dead

To repeat the principle this book was intended to convey, **only the love of God is capable of placing the one it loves on the altar.** It is still bound to be painful and frightening for those laid on the altar, but I think that if we can realize that the One who laid us on the altar loves us infinitely, if we can understand God's plan, our place in it and what lies ahead, it will be easier for us. If Job while in the midst of his story could have read chapter forty-two of the Book of Job; if Benjamin, pondering punishment and death on the way back to the city, could have imagined at least for a second what unexpected and incredible joy lay ahead for him; if Isaac could have imagined what actually would take place on Mount Moriah; if Lazarus and his sisters could have known what the Lord had prepared for them – it probably would have been easier for them to bear their suffering. You and I have found ourselves in the middle of God's plan, both in the sense that it is not yet finished, and in the sense that Israel is at its center. The glorious end, which Genesis chapter forty-five, Job chapter forty-two, and chapter eleven, verse forty-three of John point to, still lays ahead for us. Perhaps you do not always find within yourself the strength to believe in all those prophecies and promises to Israel which sound so unrealistic and improbable in the face of our current reality. If so, then flip back through the pages of this book, or better yet through the pages of the Bible stories themselves. Remember Job and Lazarus who felt forsaken by God, remember their seemingly hopeless situations, and remember the finales of those

---

[372] Gen. 22:8, author's translation

stories. This is how it will be for us. I don't know what Isaac was thinking while he was lying bound on the altar, but you and I know for certain that this isn't the end of our story and that the moment will come when we will descend from the altar and walk up out of the desert, **shining with the glory of God.**

The one God has called His son and firstborn must first endure the *shame* before he can enter into His glory. Two thousand years ago when people told Yeshua, *'If You are the Son of God, come down from the cross,'*[373] He did not come down for the very reason that He **was** the Son of God. God's Son could not enter into the glory of the Father without having first *endured the cross, despising the shame.*[374] May these thoughts about the One *who endured such hostility… against Himself,*[375] as well as the title that the Lord gave me for this book, encourage all of us who weep for Israel and hurt together with these people. After crucifixion comes resurrection. That great miracle, together with the joy and glory of God, awaits the one He Himself destined to undergo suffering and death. *For if their being cast away is the reconciling of the world, what will their acceptance be but **life from the dead?**[376]

---

[373] Mat. 27:40
[374] Heb. 12:2
[375] Heb. 12:3
[376] Rom. 11:15

FOR JERUSALEM

See, I have inscribed you on the palms of My hands;
Your walls are continually before Me. (Is. 49.16)

When the tumult was stilled across the land,
Silent tears the only trace of her wails,
Your walls, forever engraved on My hand,
Prepared to be pierced by the nails.

Muffled cries break through the morning calm:
Blood streamed down that Passover Eve;
And the nail that was thrust into My living palm
An eternal imprint would leave…

In the sun's blackened glare, sightless man could not see,
To the blind to perceive was not given,
That in pounding that nail to the cross first through Me,
Into your walls it was driven.

❃ ❃ ❃

Having now risen, I still bear the stain
Of those marks bestowed then by mankind;
On the palms of My hands your walls yet remain:
With those old rusty scars you're aligned.

Full of envy and spite, and indifferent to them,
No wounds the blind world recalls,
Driving those same ancient nails, O Jerusalem,
Fearlessly into your walls.

And once again, they know not what they do
To Me, Who sees all whence I stand:
Every time that they target your walls, they renew
The pain in the palm of My hand.

Made in the USA
Columbia, SC
01 February 2019